All the Way Home:
Aging in Haiku

Also by Robert Epstein:

A Congregation of Cows: Moo Haiku

A Walk around Spring Lake: Haiku

(Editor) *Beyond the Grave: Contemporary Afterlife Haiku*

Checkout Time is Noon: Death Awareness Haiku

Checkout Time is Soon: More Death Awareness Haiku

(Editor) *Devastating Wisdom: The Radical Teachings of U.G. Krishnamurti*

(Editor) *Dreams Wander On: Contemporary Poems of Death Awareness*

(Co-Editor with Miriam Wald) *Every Chicken, Cow, Fish and Frog: Animal Rights Haiku*

Free to Dance Forever: Mourning Haiku for My Mother

Haiku Days of Remembrance: In Honor of My Father

Haiku Edge: New and Selected Poems

Haiku Forest Afterlife

Healing into Haiku: On Illness and Pain

(Second author with Stacy Taylor) *Living Well with a Hidden Disability*

Nothing is Empty: A Whole Haiku World

(Editor) *Now This: Contemporary Poems of Beginnings, Renewals, and Firsts*

(With Stacy Taylor) *Suffering Buddha: The Zen Way Beyond Health and Illness*

(Editor) *The Breath of Surrender: A Collection of Recovery-Oriented Haiku*

(Compiler with Sherry Phillips) *The Natural Man: A Thoreau Anthology*

(Editor) *The Quotable Krishnamurti*

Reckoning with Winter: A Haiku Hailstorm

(Editor) *The Sacred in Contemporary Haiku*

(Editor) *The Temple Bell Stops: Contemporary Poems of Grief, Loss and Change*

(Editor) *They Gave Us Life: Celebrating Mothers, Fathers, & Others in Haiku*

Turkey Heaven: Animal Rights Haiku

Turning the Page to Old: Haiku & Senryu

What My Niece Said in My Head: Haiku & Senryu

All the Way Home:
Aging in Haiku

Edited by
Robert Epstein

2019

All the Way Home: Aging in Haiku
Copyright © 2019 Robert Epstein
All rights reserved.

ISBN 978-1-7341254-2-9

Cover image in the public domain;
gratefully accessed at www.pixabay.com

Middle Island Press
PO Box 354
West Union WV 26456

I love living. I love that I'm alive to love my age.

~ *Maya Angelou*

The older I get, the greater power I have to help the world; I am like a snowball – the further I am rolled the more I gain.

~ *Susan B. Anthony*

Grow old along with me! The best is yet to be.

~ *Robert Browning*

You can't help getting older, but you don't have to get old.

~ *George Burns*

Old age is no place for sissies.

~ *Betty Davis*

We turn not older with years but newer every day.

~ *Emily Dickinson*

Do not grow old, no matter how long you live. Never cease to stand like curious children before the great mystery into which we were born.

~ *Albert Einstein*

Getting older, you refuse to fritter away your time on nonsense. You drop your masks, your little vanities and false ambitions.

~ *T. S. Eliot*

The years teach much which the days never knew.

~ *Ralph Waldo Emerson*

Anyone who stops learning is old, whether at twenty or eighty.

~ *Henry Ford*

Those who love deeply never grow old; they may die of old age, but they die young.

~ *Benjamin Franklin*

Aging is not 'lost youth' but a new stage of opportunity and strength.

~ *Betty Friedan*

The afternoon knows what the morning never suspected.

~ *Robert Frost*

Of all the self-fulfilling prophecies in our culture the assumption that aging means decline and poor health is probably the deadliest.

~ *Marilyn Ferguson*

For the unlearned, old age is winter; for the learned, it is the season of the harvest.

~ *Hasidic saying*

As you grow older, you will discover that you have two hands, one for helping yourself, the other for helping others.

~ *Audrey Hepburn*

To be seventy years young is sometimes far more cheerful and hopeful than to be forty years old.

~ *Oliver Wendell Holmes*

The greatest potential for growth and self-realisation exists in the second half of life.

~ *Carl Jung*

Anyone who keeps the ability to see beauty never grows old.

~ *Franz Kafka*

At age 20, we worry about what others think of us. At 40, we don't care what they think of us. At 60, we discover they haven't been thinking of us at all.

~ *Ann Landers*

Count your age by friends, not years.

~ *John Lennon*

In the end, it's not the years in your life that count. It's the life in your years.

~ *Abraham Lincoln*

Age has no reality except in the physical world.

~ *Gabriel Garcia Marquez*

Getting older is no problem. You just have to live long enough.

~ *Groucho Marx*

If you associate enough with older people who do enjoy their lives, who are not stored away in any golden ghettos, you will gain a sense of continuity and of the possibility for a full life.

~ *Margaret Mead*

To know how to grow old is the master work of wisdom, and one of the most difficult chapters in the great art of living.

~ *Herman Melville*

I want to grow old without facelifts. . . I want to have the courage to be loyal to the face I've made.

~ *Marilyn Monroe*

Time may be a great healer, but a lousy beautician.

~ *Dorothy Parker*

As one grows old, life and art become one and the same.

~ *Pablo Picasso*

I believe in old age; to work and to grow old: this is what life expects of us.

~ *Rainer Maria Rilke*

Beautiful young people are accidents of nature, but beautiful old people are works of art.

~ *Eleanor Roosevelt*

Do not deprive me of my age. I have earned it.

~ *May Sarton*

You don't stop laughing when you grow old, you grow old when you stop laughing.

~ *George Bernard Shaw*

With age comes the inner, the higher life. Who would be forever young, to dwell always in externals?

~ *Elizabeth Cady Stanton*

None are so old as those who have outlived enthusiasm.

~ *Henry D. Thoreau*

The biggest surprise in a man's life is old age.

~ *Leo Tolstoy*

Age is an issue of mind over matter. If you don't mind, it doesn't matter.

~ *Mark Twain*

. . . one can remain alive long past the date of disintegration if one is unafraid of change, insatiable in intellectual curiosity, interested in big things, and happy in small ways.

~ *Edith Wharton*

Wisdom comes with winters.

~ *Oscar Wilde*

I don't believe in aging. I believe in forever altering one's aspect to the sun.

~ *Virginia Woolf*

The wiser mind mourns less for what age takes away than what it leaves behind.

~ *William Wordsworth*

The longer I live the more beautiful life becomes.

~ *Frank Lloyd Wright*

Dedicated to. . .

Liz Kamens

and to

Lucas Nicolosi

born 27 July 2019

Table of Contents

Acknowledgments	xiii
Introduction	xv
Poems	1
Glossary	309
Recommended Reading	311

Acknowledgments

I am always happy to express appreciation for family and friends: Janet Amptman, Kathy DiNapoli, David J. and Nancy Eagle, Debbie Edwards, Martin Epstein, Clara Knopfler, Joy McCall, Sherry Phillips, Judy Rader, Rocco Randazzo, David H. Rosen, Wendy Etsuko Siu, Lillian Schwartz, and Joan Vander Ryk, Sophie Solani. Jay Schlesinger, Stacy Taylor and Miriam Wald—in whom I have confided for so many years—deserve my deepest gratitude.

I want to acknowledge Joy McCall and to thank Shelley Baker-Gard with the Portland Haiku Group for their help in circulating the call for submissions. Zee Zahava, who maintains a haiku blog online, was very helpful in providing contact information for several poets; her women-only haiku blog is: www.brassbellhaiku.blogspot.com.

Thanks also to Katharine Allard of the New Zealand Haiku Society. I am likewise very grateful to Ignatius Fay, the electronic editor of the Haiku Society of America's Newsletter, for posting the call for submissions in the monthly HSA Newsletter. In addition, I am extremely grateful to Dianne Garcia, HSA Secretary, who graciously assisted with contact information for a number of contributors as well as to John Stevenson, managing editor of *The Heron's Nest*. Editor Wanda D. Cook deserves thanks for posting a call in her *New England Letters*.

Last but not least, I bow deeply to Christina Taylor at Middle Island Press for once again helping in her inimitable way to bring another haiku project into the light of day.

Introduction

> From the middle of life onward, only he [or she]
> remains vitally alive who is ready to die with life.
>
> ~ *Carl Jung*

It is no easy task to honor the *full-catastrophe* of life without falling either into despair or sentimentality. The truth is aging can be characterized as neither good nor bad; *it just is*. I recall so clearly how my dear grandmother—who died a few months before her 96th birthday—would occasionally observe, almost as a third-party witness, "the age is there." At other times, perhaps when her arthritis flared in her hands or hip, she would lament: "Getting old is for the birds." According to my aunt, my grandmother also referred to herself in her later years as "a soup chicken," which she distinguished from "a spring chicken." I like to think there is room for all these reactions and more.

I am not sure how the birds feel about aging, but none of us is exempt, including the trees, bees and even stone walls. So, it is best, I think, to lean into the existential reality of change in order to discern what Nature has to teach or communicate to us. At the same time, this is not an invitation to morbid ruminating, insists Thomas Moore, author of *Ageless Soul: The Lifelong Journey Toward Meaning and Joy*. "Aging is a fact of life, Moore affirms. "You might want to honor it and reflect on it, but you don't need to be obsessed by it." p. 21

Is it possible not only to avoid obsessing about aging, but to also resist the temptation to idealize it, as many have done in glorifying the so-called "golden years"? There is a movement currently afoot to "disrupt" the myths and stereotypes associated with aging.

While this is generally a healthy impulse—especially insofar as it combats bias and discrimination—I am concerned that there may be an element of denial as well as idealization interwoven into the well-intentioned effort to rescue aging from devaluation. (See **Senior Bypassing** below.) Poet and fellow contributor, Naomi Wakan, whose emotional honesty I greatly appreciate, shares her real-life experience of aging in *A Roller Coaster Ride: Thoughts on Aging* which, I suspect, is very common:

> Though I am in my eighties now, I do not seem to have moved into the calm and wisdom that people promised me old age would bring. My life is more like a roller coaster. Some days I feel totally part of the universe. Life seems interconnected and meaningful and the words flow from me as if coming from a deep source. Death slots in naturally as all things come into being and pass away. Other times everything falls to pieces. The world outside seems menacing and fearful and death a losing game. p. 9

Aging is important not only because it instigates a confrontation with our finiteness but also serves as a means for integrating death into our lives. The awareness of aging throws loss into ever sharper relief, as it were, so that we can observe more intently what it means to die to everything, here-and-now, over and over again, as the spiritual teacher, J. Krishnamurti, urges. And, as Zen teacher, Shunryu Suzuki asserts in *Zen Mind, Beginner's Mind*:

> We should be very grateful to have a limited body... like mine, or like yours. If you had a limitless life it would be a real problem for you. p. 10

Youth afforded us the opportunity to immerse ourselves actively and passionately in life; aging does not do the opposite. Rather, aging encourages one to redirect the passion of youth inward for the purpose of *seeing through the illusion of separateness*. Everything we are taught from the earliest age emphasizes the vital importance of an individual identity and we set about attaining this for the better part of one's adult life. In stark contrast to the lifelong pursuit of self-actualization, the great realization of aging is the way in which all of us and all things return to the Earth from which we originated. This is a holy truth that can only be apprehended through a medium attuned to truth, and haiku poetry (and its related forms) is a compelling vehicle for truth.

The fact that aging is associated with change and loss need not plunge one into sorrow or regret. There are permutations which, from virtually any angle, may be viewed as progress, improvement, refinement. Lewis Richmond, author of *Aging as a Spiritual Practice: A Contemplative Guide to Growing Older and Wiser*, stresses this important point:

> "Everything changes," yes, but that truth has two sides. It is true that everything we love is destined to change, age, and pass away. But it is equally true that every moment brings with it new possibilities. We shouldn't allow our fixed ideas about aging to take those opportunities away. p. 9

Aren't some forms of aging likened to fine wines, whose taste becomes more agreeable, if not elegant and sublime, over time? Carl Jung, the Swiss psychiatrist who broke with Freud to found his own spiritually-oriented psychotherapy approach, is convinced that aging has a purpose beyond simply living to a ripe, old age. In a thought-provoking paper entitled, "Stages of Life," which appears in *Modern Man in Search of a Soul*, he writes:

A human being would certainly not grow to be seventy or eighty years old if this longevity had no meaning for the species. The afternoon of human life . . . has a significance of its own.

Jung passionately maintained that aging does not, as a general rule, lead headlong into steep decline. Writing in *Jung and Aging*, Leslie Sawin emphasizes Jung's strength-based view of aging, which draws on the latter's aforementioned paper of 1930:

He believed that psychological and spiritual growth is possible at every age and often continues into very old age. So to think of aging as a period of relentless decline is a mistake. In fact, much current research supports the possibility of continuing growth and development during old age and, therefore, the premise that one can grow into old age rather than sink into it. (p. 20) For Jung, old age was a summons to internal growth and personality development, and it provided the opportunity to enrich life, deepen spirituality, and define a new sense of meaning. p. 10

Looking back, I remembered how depressed I found myself at the (perceived) loss of youth when I turned thirty (!). The therapist I was seeing at the time countered with a bit of wisdom that has remained with me for more than forty years: "There is beauty at every age." And so it is.

Beauty, of course, isn't the only quality that endures through the corridors of time. The same could be said of many other qualities, including: courage, determination, wisdom, creativity, fortitude, perseverance, resilience, open-heartedness, patience, compassion, maturity, faith—to name but a few. The ancient Chinese sage, Lao

Tzu, has this to say about the value of aging in *The Tao Te Ching*, heralding grandmothers:

> When you realize where you come from,
> you naturally become tolerant,
> disinterested, amused,
> kindhearted as a grandmother...

A Broader Perspective

What is haiku—and its related forms—for? Haiku is for sharing, as the late haiku poet and scholar, William J. Higginson, proposed. If haiku is for sharing, then it is also for friendship, as a psychotherapy client and fellow poet astutely observed.

What is aging for? I suggest that, taking a broader view, *aging is for liberation*. Liberation is for *being*; that is, living fully and freely in harmony with Nature. You may think that liberation comes at the very end of your life, but that is not my understanding. True freedom or liberation is *right here, right now* in the very midst of aging.

In this light, J. Krishnamurti[1] asks some difficult questions in a talk he gave in Bombay in February, 1957:

> What do you mean by old age? Going bald, losing one's teeth? The physical organism inevitably wears itself out through long use. Is that old age? Or is old age the deterioration of the mind? You may be very young, healthy, strong, and yet be old because your mind is already on the path of deterioration.

Krishnamurti continues:

So what do we mean by old age? Surely we are not talking of the gradual wearing out of the body through use and decay. We do not mean that. We mean the state of the mind which has grown old because it has no innocence. Do you understand, sir? The mind is old when it is not fresh, when it is always thinking in terms of the past and using the present as a passage to the future. It is such a mind that is not young. And can such a mind be made new, innocent, fresh? Can it renew itself from moment to moment so that it never grows old? Surely that is our problem, not how to stop the aging of the body, which is of course impossible.

From the perspective of poets included in these pages, aging and its relation to innocence may be understood in many ways. At the risk of oversimplifying, a number of broad themes have emerged, which I briefly enumerate below. I hasten to add that there are a number of other possibilities for making sense out of the contributors' insights and observations, and I encourage the reader to be on the lookout for such alternatives when contemplating the art and poems in this collection.

Consolidating/Releasing

Aging may be viewed as a process of consolidating what one has learned and experienced over the course of a lifetime. For some, consolidating knowledge, insight, wisdom, creativity, wealth, reputation and the like may serve the purpose of *solidifying* one's sense of self or place in the world. Solidifying the self may offset the existential reality that life is impermanent: Even though human beings die, it is possible to leave something behind that testifies to our having lived. This is why many people take care to preserve their legacy, which typically takes the form of a last will and testament, but may manifest in other ways as well which existential psychiatrist, Irvin Yalom, calls "rippling"[(2)]; e.g., planting a garden or tree; installing a park bench with the donor's name on a plaque; imparting wisdom through a book of poetry.

Consolidating only constitutes one half of aging. For others, who feel less impelled to preserve a sense of self, the focus may turn more to releasing. The experience of releasing or letting go is liberating: A great deal of energy in life is bound up with collecting things such as possessions, degrees, credentials, titles; and one may realize that all this accumulation matters much less in one's later years. I once saw a bumper sticker that encapsulated the essence of this shift in priorities: THE MOST PRECIOUS THINGS IN LIFE AREN'T THINGS. People begin to dispose of books, photographs, clothing and the like. Things may be whittled down to prized possessions such as a necklace or watch that belonged to one's great grandparent. My dear mother who died at the age of 92 cherished a doll her aunt had given to her when she was five; she kept it neatly in the top drawer of her dresser until the day she died.

Expanding/Contracting

As I have suggested, aging can be characterized, in part, as a process of consolidating and releasing. There is a noteworthy variation of this dynamic which might be called expanding and contracting.

An older person may expand his/her life by returning to a hobby or craft that previously occupied his or her attention. Or, with more free time gained by retirement, one may pursue a newfound or lifelong interest such as writing, gardening, or guitar playing. Becoming actively involved in the rearing of grandchildren out of love or practical necessity may similarly be seen as an expansion.

Undertaking travel adventures with a spouse, friends, or group for personal enrichment or building international bridges likewise falls into the expanding category.

Naturally, not everyone has the energy, motivation or interest in expanding. Perhaps due to cognitive/physical decline or lack of interest, some people withdraw or contract as they age. This is not necessarily cause for concern, nor should contracting be automatically labeled abnormal. Each of us has the right to choose the extent to which we engage in inward or outward journeys in our later years.

Looking Back/Looking Forward

Of course, one is always free to pause and look back from whence one came. In reality, competitively-oriented cultures tend to be future-oriented. With the thrust of their momentum centered on what comes next, many people don't even think to catch their breath and reflect on where they have been. This drivenness is what prompted John Lennon to wake people up with the poignant line that appears in two of his later songs: "Life is what's happening/as you're busy making other plans."

As one begins to slow down later in life, there may be a desire to stop and reminisce. This is especially true when one realizes that there is more life behind him or her than remains to be lived. In nursing homes, facilitators offer workshops called Life Reviews where participants are asked a series of prompts that stimulate self-reflection about the past. In this connection, nostalgia is a cognitive tool of recovery. It is akin to a flashback, which is aversive in the case of trauma, but comforting or bittersweet when the memory recovered transports one back, for example, to a time of youthful love. Engaging in nostalgia or life review is likely to be evocative, calling up memories of past loves; pride of accomplishment; as well as losses, mistakes, and mishaps.

Aging, however, is not a cataclysmic fall off the edge of a cliff. Even those who are at an advanced age have things they may be looking forward to, including their next meal or a visit with an adult child or grandchild. Such is the nature of being alive. My 92 year old aunt who survived the Holocaust with her beloved mother, continues to be excited by invitations to speak to any group—young or old—about the horrors of Nazism. Her mission is to educate anyone willing to listen to her urgent message: *never forget.*

Change/Loss

Beyond the bodily changes which accompany aging, we lose beloved parents and relatives, spouses and partners, friends, and colleagues. While the death of loved ones can occur at any phase of life, these losses multiply in midlife and beyond. Grief and sorrow become an inescapable part of aging. More than a few poets sent me many beautiful and poignant haiku relating to grief and mourning. I have only included a sampling of poems on bereavement, because I dedicated a separate haiku anthology to the theme of grief and loss, *The Temple Bell Stops: Contemporary Poems of Grief, Loss and Change.*

Of course, despite the changes and losses—both internal and external—associated with aging, growing old is not only about decline and deterioration. A good many older adults continue to learn, which leads to the acquisition of new knowledge, skills and abilities. Retirees may resolve to reinvent themselves after retirement by enrolling in a foreign language class or volunteering to help refugees get settled in the community.

While old friends and family members pass away, those who are social and outgoing may make new friends at a senior center memoir writing group or a weekly folk dancing class. Numerous other examples abound.

Memory loss preoccupies many people. Too often, one's sense of self is bound up with the ability to recall names and words for use in communication as well as images and past experiences. Spiritually speaking, we are not what we remember but the conditioned mind tends to believe otherwise.

Do the changes related to aging signify imperfections that we need to hide at all costs? I appreciate what meditation teacher, Jack Kornfield invites the reader to do in *No Time Like the Present*:

> If you want to explore imperfections and love, take off your clothes and look into a full-length mirror. Notice the mysterious gifts of having a human body and a human life. And notice all the ideas of how it should be. Can you see and love your body, and your human life, clearly as it is? With all its unique messy, wild, uncharted, imperfect glory? p. 140

Although human beings face change and loss throughout their lives—some more than others—change and loss accelerate as we age. We retire from a job we loved or hated; there are changes that we notice in mind or body; and, if we live long enough, friends, family, and former coworkers or neighbors pass away.

One of the greatest challenges in life is how to respond to these multiple losses. Each loss gives rise to a different course of mourning so there is no predetermined map for grieving. Still, it behooves us to remain as conscious as we can in regards to the way in which we respond to the many losses we experience in life.

Depending on one's overall mental/emotional well-being, we may respond with resilience or rigidity. For some, the amount of loss may be come overwhelming to the point where the older adult shuts down. Depression is not uncommon in seniors, and a few close their hearts and descend into bitterness, feeling like it is all too much to bear.

Belonging/Loneliness

Many social scientists consider human beings to be social animals which, generally speaking, means that we like to affiliate with others. Of course, depending on temperament, personality and life experience, some people are more—or less—inclined to seek a sense of belonging through family ties, friendships, social groups, religious or spiritual traditions, political organizations, and the arts.

Belonging helps to preserve a sense of individual identity, continuity, and emotional stability; in short, a feeling of being rooted. For older adults who have lost friends and family as well as other social contacts for any number of reasons—infirmity, estrangement, diminishing mobility—a cloud of loneliness and social withdrawal may descend upon them. This isolation may trigger anxiety, depression, or even despair, which might call for the assistance of a mental health professional and/or other social services.

Twilight/Beyond

Coming to terms with one's own mortality is the work of a lifetime. Sensitive and curious children may awaken to the reality of death early in life, but the imminence of death looms large the older we get. Jean Jacques Rousseau, the 18th century iconoclastic writer and author of *Reveries of a Solitary Walker*, believed that the old are, indeed, capable of learning and ought to turn their attention to the imminent task at hand:

> If an old man [or woman] has something to learn, it is the art of dying, and this is precisely what occupies people least at my age; we think of anything rather that that. Quoted in Wakan, p. 175

To contemplate our finiteness as well as the afterlife is not in any way morbid. As the Buddha taught:

> Of all footprints
> that of the elephant is supreme.
> Of all mindfulness meditations
> that on death is supreme.

While death and the hereafter loom large later in life, I have only included a sampling of such poems in these pages. This is not due to bias, negligence, or aversion on my part. On the contrary, I have edited two entire anthologies on these very themes and refer the interested reader to them for further exploration: *Dreams Wander On: Contemporary Poems of Death Awareness* and *Beyond the Grave: Contemporary Afterlife Haiku*.

Senior Bypassing: A Cautionary Note

Aging, then, is a fact of life we can either accept or deny and resist.

The latter appears to be an unskillful response to reality.

While it is true that some people succumb to despair when they reach a certain age, believing that their life is now over, it is no less true that denying the reality of aging may lead to a form of delusion, which is problematic, too.

A recent movement facilitated by AARP, an organization founded to promote health and well-being of older adults, is dedicated to "disrupting" aging. The rationale for the movement centers around challenging distortions and prejudices associated with growing old.

However well-intentioned this undertaking is, I am concerned that it may perpetuate denial on a subtle level while reinforcing the preoccupation with youth in the process. For the indisputable fact is that humans *do* age; our bodies and minds *do* undergo changes that include decrements and loss in varying degrees.

Consequently, I believe it is more skillful and adaptive to acknowledge the truth about aging. Insofar as haiku—and its related forms—is exquisitely suited to revelations of truth, I have turned to this medium for an exploration of the myriad ways in which human beings age.

Transpersonal psychologist, John Welwood, coined the term "spiritual bypassing" to refer to attempts by spiritual seekers to avoid working through psychological conflicts by immersing themselves in religious pursuits like meditation, chanting, or yoga. However, such efforts to *bypass* these inner struggles don't work in the long run; they eventually resurface because suppression or sublimation does not facilitate inner healing.

I believe something akin to spiritual bypassing occurs in those who deny the reality of aging or endeavor to suppress its manifestations that include love handles, wrinkles, and hair loss. Therefore, I would like to propose a term that similarly points to a parallel process of denial; let's call it *senior bypassing*, which may be seen in over-reliance on Botox treatments, face lifts and attire meant to be worn by teenagers or young adults, rather than by those over 55.

If denial is not a resilient way to face aging, what is? One might be tempted to say that acceptance is the healthy alternative. Acceptance is certainly an improvement, but something more is still called for, I believe. What I envision beyond acceptance is the *embodied realization* that our aging organism is a part of the very Earth from which we arose and to which we return. This goes to the heart of what the secular teacher, J. Krishnamurti, means when he observes: "you are the world." Like Nature itself, we embody the seasons as well as the movement of life-and-death: There is a budding, a flowering, a withering and a dying which eventually starts anew.

Conclusion

As the great American satirist, Mark Twain, remarked: "Do not complain about growing old. It is a privilege denied to many." That is, for those of us fortunate enough to survive illness, accident, and tragedy earlier in life, we will have to face old age with all its vicissitudes. However, I respectfully disagree with Twain in regards to complaining, as I view the latter as a legitimate form of coping (so long as it does not become the *sole* means of dealing with life's stresses and strains).

Still, it may help to remember that aging is a natural and inevitable part of life and the contributors in this volume unequivocally attest to that. Most do so by situating aging within the larger context of Nature. For all our scientific and technological advances, human beings still arise from, and return to, the Earth. Knowing I am an integral part of the natural world—along with wolves, redwoods, pelicans, and vast bodies of water—consoles me when I am beset by aches, pains and a general loss of stamina. I look around and behold that everything grows old and dies, eventually.

Appreciating our roots in the natural world is what Ram Dass, a longtime meditation teacher and Hindu devotee, urges us to do. Writing in *Still Here: Embracing Aging, Changing and Dying*, his words frame much of the poetry and art found in these pages:

> The body and its aging journey can be viewed from a larger perspective. When we look at the shifts in our physical state from a Soul perspective, the difference is remarkable: instead of bemoaning the loss of who we were, we marvel at who we are becoming. If we know that we are more than the body, we're free to relate to it less fearfully, with mercy, instead of resentment, toward its aches and pains. Seeing the body as a part of nature, we do not fear the signs of death in quite the same way as before. We may even learn to love our bodies, and to appreciate their different beauty, as they change from young to old. p. 68

Life is not a cruel joke (though it may seem this way in the face of adversity or great loss); it is, in reality, a precious incarnation, as mindfulness meditation teacher, Joseph Goldstein, has called it, and the contributors in these pages have bequeathed to us all their impassioned testimonials to this holy truth. Please know that you are not walking all the way home alone. Let me leave you with these words by the poet Rainer Maria Rilke from his *Book of Hours: Love Poems to God*:

> . . . you are not too old
> and it is not too late
> to dive into your increasing depths
> where life calmly gives out
> its own secret.

Notes

[1] J. Krishnamurti. Fourth Public Talk in Bombay, 20 February 1957; accessed 8/6/19 online at: http://jiddu-krishnamurti.net/en/1957/1957-02-20-jiddu-krishnamurti-4thpublic-talk.

[2] See Irvin D. Yalom, *Staring at the Sun: Overcoming the Terror of Death*. San Francisco, CA: Jossey-Bass, 2008.

Robert Epstein
El Cerrito, CA
24 August 2019

Poems

walking
the paths we used
to run

    ~odd g. aksnes, *The Heron's Nest*, 19, 2017

vacant nest
how empty the house —
back to our beginning

    ~Adjei Agyei-Baah

Father's Day
all that he asks for
a pipe and an easy chair

    ~Adjei Agyei-Baah, *Afriku: Haiku and Senryu from Ghana*, 2016

voter's line . . .
an old man naps
on his walking stick

   ~*Adjei Agyei-Baah, AQ,* 2018

old mattress
mother sinks deeper
than I

   ~ *Adjei Agyei-Baah, cattails,* 2018

aged couple
renewing their vows
wordlessly

   ~*Adjei Agyei-Baah, IRIS International Haiku Magazine,* 2018

a bird
from the thinning trees...
that song you once sang

    ~*Mary Frederick Ahearn, Modern Haiku,* 50.1, 2019

snowdrops
at the old place
bloom for someone else

    ~*Mary Frederick Ahearn, Acorn,* #40, 2018

faded photographs
falling for you
all over again

    ~*Mary Frederick Ahearn, Frogpond,* 42:1, 2019

cataracts he moves closer to tell me

~*frances angela, Modern Haiku, 44.2, 2013*

girlhood friend
the stories we tell
her grandchildren

~*frances angela, Blithe Spirit, 24:1, 2014*

she remembers my childhood mother's day

~*frances angela, Blithe Spirit, 26:2, 2016*

sagging breasts her eyes closed as she smiles

~*frances angela, Lilliput Review, #197, 2016*

old age marking grandma's words

   ~ frances angela

birdsoft chatter
on a summer's dawn
the old crone
wakes to dance again
arm in arm with loneliness

   ~Jenny Ward Angyal

the name
my newborn grandson shares
with a grandfather
I never knew . . .
leaves rustle in the wind

   ~Jenny Ward Angyal

finding I've shrunk
by an inch and a half . . .
yet the mountains
of my inner island
still converse with sky

   ~Jenny Ward Angyal, hedgerow, #122, 2017

squeezing shampoo
into the palm of my hand . . .
every day
a rain of blessings
over this aging body

   ~Jenny Ward Angyal, Stanford Goldstein International Tanka Contest, 2017; Honorable Mention

change your clocks
change your batteries –
how much longer
until I fall back
into that good night

   ~*Jenny Ward Angyal, A Hundred Gourds*, 3:2, 2014

thumbing through
an old rolodex
winter light

   ~*Debbi Antebi, Frogpond,* 41:3, 2018

~ an'ya, *dailyhaiga*, 2010

~an'ya, daily haiga, 2010

the good old days
when life was still simple
to contemplate
and cross-legged we sat
in a field of clover

an'ya

~ an'ya

embarking
on the final Voyage
of our lives

so much more we know now
we knew not before love

an'ya

~an'ya

ironing
a white handkerchief
and my ancestral guilt

    ˜*Fay Aoyagi, Chrysanthemum Love,* 2003

ocean fog –
I can't recall the name
of my first lover

    ˜*Fay Aoyagi, Chrysanthemum Love,* 2003

August waves
I tell my history
to a jellyfish

    ˜*Fay Aoyagi, Chrysanthemum Love,* 2003

trailing an inchworm to a childhood summer

   ~Fay Aoyagi, Beyond the Reach of My
    Chopsticks, 2011

thorns of roses
I fold my past
in half

   ~Fay Aoyagi, Beyond the Reach of My
    Chopsticks, 2011

~Marilyn Ashbaugh

~ Marilyn Ashbaugh

at their favorite table
chocolate donuts and coffee
the old guys kibitzing

~Mary Jo Balistreri

fire burning low...
the old man curled
into his chair

~Mary Jo Balistreri

morning sun on stone how pleasant retirement

~Mary Jo Balistreri

winter dusk
old fingers remember
an old tune

    ~*John Barlow, The Heron's Nest*, 15, 2013

heart trouble
in the car
sneaking cheese

    ~*Caroline Giles Banks, Brussels Sprout*, 5:1, 1988

counting open lids
on the pill box
it's Wednesday

    ~*Caroline Giles Banks*, in G. Hotham, ed., *Take-Out Window: HSA Members' Anthology*, 2004

50th reunion
the photographer asks us
to lift our chins

   ~ Caroline Giles Banks, bottle rockets, #35, 2016

angiogram
my broken heart
undetected

   ~ Caroline Giles Banks, The Clay Jar: Haiku,
   Senryu and Haibun Poems, 2013

widowed
growing my hair long
the way he liked it

   ~ Caroline Giles Banks, The Clay Jar: Haiku,
   Senryu and Haibun Poems, 2013

Parkinson's gait...
the silence between
creaks in the floorboards

~*Francine Banwarth, Modern Haiku*, 50.1, 2019

forgetting to talk
about all the aches and pains
morning glories

~*Dyana Basist*

ninetieth birthday
Mary takes her new hip
for an autumn stroll

~*Dyana Basist*

his stooped torso
leans into the cypress
lengthening days

   ~Dyana Basist

heart attack
or an errant hot flash?
shooting star

   ~Dyana Basist

after all these years
our kisses deeper now
night of stars

   ~Dyana Basist

bills paid
the tiger lily
past its prime

    ~*Roberta Beary, The Unworn Necklace*, 2007

mother's hat
short years of wanting it
long years of having it

    ~*Roberta Beary, The Unworn Necklace*, 2007

children grown
the dog quieter
than the house

    ~*Roberta Beary, The Unworn Necklace*, 2007

magnifying mirror
where the wrinkles
tell bigger stories

   ~Lori Becherer

childhood Monopoly
a well-worn
Boardwalk

   ~Lori Becherer

the shelf
of family photos
bows

   ~Lori Becherer, Chrysanthemum, 21, 2017

at ninety-nine
she asks,
I'm how old?

~ *Lori Becherer*

family reunion
all the little ones
I'll never know

~ *Lori Becherer*

elder wisdom
shared with grandkids . . .
they google it

~ *Sidney Bending*

comfort food
something he can eat
with his dentures

   ~*Sidney Bending*

pumpkin harvest
the old straw-man
thinning

   ~*Jan Benson*, Croatian Pumpkim Festival
   Contest; Highly Commended, 2017

raspberries
grandbabe's
first opinion

   ~*Jan Benson, cattails*, 2015

childhood home
my concrete footprints
going nowhere

    ~*Ernest J. Berry, Getting On*, 2016

new house
we open another box
of old smells

    ~*Ernest J. Berry, Getting On*, 2016

sciatica
my china cat
keeps smiling

    ~*Ernest J. Berry, Getting On*, 2016

golden wedding
she's forgotten
my name

   ~Ernest J. Berry, Getting On, 2016

flames licking
our old love letters
curled up together

   ~Ernest J. Berry, Getting On, 2016

thrift store bookshelf
the copy I signed
for a friend

   ~Robyn Hood Black, Frogpond, 41:2, 2018

winter rain
the fine print
smaller each year

   ~Robyn Hood Black, Chrysanthemum, 11, 2012

first frost
today she misplaced
our names

   ~Robyn Hood Black, Frogpond, 42:1, 2019

years later
my Achilles heel
still just that

   ~Robyn hood Black, bottle rockets, #37, 2017

downsized—
the whole house vacuumed
from one outlet

    ~*Robyn Hood Black, Prune Juice, 16, 2015*

old lab
I wonder what
his nose sees

    ~*Meik Blöttenberger, The Heron's Nest, 19, 2017*

father's frail voice–
a stream struggles to sing
through the ice

    ~*Meik Blöttenberger*

drying lavender
no longer fluent
in my mother tongue

   ~ Meik Blöttenberger, The Heron's Nest, 19, 2017

snow in the nest—
applying online
for Medicare

   ~ Meik Blöttenberger

rain garden
the ache and joy
in my bones

   ~ Meik Blöttenberger

tops under the stars
heirs of Orpheus picking roses
in fragrant valleys

   ~Stoianka Boianova

songs of crickets
they bring back to me
my childhood family

   ~Stoianka Boianova

my 58th spring
the field of blue lupine
never gets old

   ~Kathryn Bold, Frogpond, 41:2, 2018

youth –
many summers ago
when winter was skating

   ~Adrian Bouter

aging body hills become mountains

   ~Adrian Bouter

hospital window
branches hanging low
from old snow

   ~Adrian Bouter, Stardust Haiku, #24, 2018

my parents
in our hometown
aged Gouda

~ *Adrian Bouter,*

mother by sun...
every grey hair
a silver lining

~ *Adrian Bouter*

downsizing
every touch
a memory

~ *Gordon Bradford*

nursing home mirror
that person standing there
what's her name

   ~ Gordon Bradford; for dell

cold evening
loading pillboxes
together

   ~ Gordon Bradford

old hometown
nothing looks the same
but progress

   ~ Gordon Bradford, bottle rockets, #40, 2019

old pond
reflections of turtles
all the way down

    ~*Mark E. Brager, Frogpond,* 42:1, 2019

playing catch at dusk,
I dimly remember
being the son

    ~*Mark E. Brager, Prune Juice,* #9, 2012

swimming lesson
my son floating away
from me

    ~*Mark E. Brager, haijinx,* IV:1, 2011

burning leaves
Dad still remembers
Dresden

> ~Mark E. Brager, *Frozen Butterfly*, #1, 2014

a lifetime ago white blossoms

> ~Mark E. Brager, *Frogpond*, 39:3, 2016

fragrance of rain
caught inside
a rusted bell

> ~John Brandi, *Seeding the Cosmos: New & Selected Haiku*, 2010

in the mirror
the old man I was afraid of
as a child

> ~John Brandi, *Seeding the Cosmos: New & Selected Haiku*, 2010

arranging lilacs
he discovers
an age spot

> ~John Brandi, *Seeding the Cosmos: New & Selected Haiku*, 2010

too old
for the haircut
the stylist offers

> ~John Brandi, *Seeding the Cosmos: New & Selected Haiku*, 2010

thinking of retirement
he realizes
he never had a job

> ~John Brandi, *Seeding the Cosmos: New & Selected Haiku*, 2010

nursing home garden
the Kansas wind tousles
his thin hair

> ~*Randy Brooks,* in N. M. Sola, ed. *Four Hundred and Two Snails: 2018 HSA Members' Anthology*

moonlit patio
a pair of old sneakers
spooning

> ~*Helen Buckingham, Modern Haiku,* 50.1, 2019

chestnut moon
the eldest resident
lights up

> ~*Helen Buckingham*, Seinen-jo Maple Moon Award, 2012; Commended; also in *sanguinella*, 2017

weighing dad sparrow-light the needle flies west

> ~*Helen Buckingham, Bones*, 5, 2014; also in *sanguinella*, 2017

sleep
ever slower
to download

> ~*Helen Buckingham, Otata*, 29, 2018

old as the crow flies

~*Helen Buckingham, Acorn,* #40, 2018

in the water
under an old bridge
an old bicycle

~*Owen Bullock, breakfast with epiphanies*, 2012

after all these years
bent with longing
I assume
the half lotus

~*Owen Bullock, breakfast with epiphanies*, 2012

three kingfishers
in and out
the old mine shaft

    ~*Owen Bullock, breakfast with epiphanies,* 2012

44
on the swing
with my ice cream

    ~*Owen Bullock, breakfast with epiphanies,* 2012

even now I decide
not to cross out
mother's number

    ~*Owen Bullock, breakfast with epiphanies,* 2012

getting old—
   I fill my pill box
   with sighs

   ~Susan Burch

Same old excuses
my heart is a no-show

   ~Merle Burgess, in N. M. Sola, ed. *Four Hundred and Two Snails: HSA Members' Anthology,* 2018

those few leaves
left on the apple tree
old friends

   ~Sondra J. Byrnes, *Modern Haiku,* 50.1, 2019

the wood fence
graying in the sun
doggy's muzzle

   ~ *Claire Vogel Camargo*

the smell
of clean linens
decades old

   ~ *Claire Vogel Camargo*

chocolate chip
cookies from an old tin
grandma's ring

   ~ *Claire Vogel Camargo, Blue Hole: A Magazine of the Georgetown Poetry Festival,* 2017

summer
35 years since she held
white camellias

~ Claire Vogel Camargo, Blithe Spirit, 28:4, 2018

assimilating   into senior living

mom

~ Claire Vogel Camargo, cattails, 2018

candles flare—
yet another birthday
without mother's song

   ~ Pris Campbell

old friend
we share stories of sore bones
and once hunky men

   ~ Pris Campbell

misty window...
the kid makes snow angels
like I once did

   ~ Pris Campbell

golden years
this boy I could have kissed
calls me ma'am

   ~ Pris Campbell

clearing out 'stuff'...
found in my old bell bottoms,
his faded love note

   ~ Pris Campbell

Grandpa's watch
the face and hands
I've never known

   ~ Theresa A. Cancro, Mayfly, 65, 2018

cataracts
the blur of names
that is high school

   ~ Theresa A. Cancro

chin hair –
a dandelion missed
by the mower

   ~ Theresa A. Cancro, cattails, 2016

sickle moon's edge of my menopause

   ~ Theresa A. Cancro, #FemkuMag, #10, 2019

fall frost —
all their love letters
tightly bound

~*Theresa A. Cancro, Presence, #53, 2015*

mud wasps
the soft crumble
of time

~*Matthew Caretti, The Heron's Nest, 18, 2016*

approaching fifty
on balance
mountain and sky

~*Matthew Caretti*

Central Park
a veteran's war story
still raw

~ *Yu Chang, Modern Haiku, 48.1, 2017*

old barn
a pine eye
lets in the sun

~ *Yu Chang, The Heron's Nest, 19, 2017*

Christmas tree
steps of the ladder
seem steeper

~ *Marta Chocilowska*

old couple
sipping chilli chocolate
from same cup

~*Marta Chocilowska*

silver wedding . . .
taste of the wild raspberries
still sweet and tart

~*Marta Chocilowska,* The 28th ITO EN Oi Ocha New Haiku Contest, 2017; Merit Award

hometown
a glass skyscraper mirrors
the old sakura

~*Marta Chocilowska,* Vancouver Cherry Blossom Festival, 2018; International Sakura Award

white chrysanthemum
who will remember me
when I'm gone

   ~Marta Chocilowska, in Z. Zahava, ed. *brass bell,* 2013

stalking the heron
old man in a black beret
aims his zoom lens

   ~Margaret Chula, Grinding My Ink, 1993

old woman
and lotus leaves
bow low to the pond

   ~Margaret Chula, Grinding My Ink, 1993

sultry afternoon
in Grandma's junk mail
Fredericks of Hollywood

~ *Margaret Chula, The Smell of Rust*, 2003

nursing home
she rubs my lipstick kiss
into her cheeks

~ *Margaret Chula, The Smell of Rust*, 2003

catalpa blossoms—
falling in love with
the girl I once was

~ Margaret Chula, *The Smell of Rust*, 2003

Sicilian spring—
old women's voices
drill ancient stone

~*Rick Clark*

in a cloudy window
a homeless man strokes
his long white beard

~*Rick Clark*

the retired men
sitting beside the green lake—
talking plumbing

~*Rick Clark*

the last straw
the white hair on my foot—
yoga stretch

    ~ Rick Clark

we ask grandma
if we can feel her wings—
so soft!

    ~ Rick Clark

our checkered past—
colorful leaves carpet
the rainy path

    ~ Tom Clausen, Frogpond, 42:1, 2019

standing at this window
I remember mother
standing here

   ~ *Tom Clausen, Laughing at Myself,* 2013

those were the days. . .
She'd meet me halfway
from work

   ~ *Tom Clausen, Laughing at Myself,* 2013

framed photo—
the three of us
close back then

   ~ *Tom Clausen, Laughing at Myself,* 2013

back home
the old truck comes to rest
in its ruts

~*Tom Clausen, Laughing at Myself,* 2013

snow on the lake
memories I pull
from the deep

~*Glenn G. Coats, The Heron's Nest,* 15, 2013

the way hands
remember the chords
first love

~*Glenn G. Coats, The Heron's Nest,* 19, 2017

Buckled teak house –greyed by time
A woman plants rice –bent with age

   ~*Julie Constable*

Rusted cars, bleached grass
Peeling weatherboards
It's not a 'tidy town'

   ~*Julie Constable*

three generations
in the patchwork quilt
autumn leaves

   ~*Susan Constable, Autumn Moon*, 2:1, 2018;
   Runner-Up, *Best of Autumn Moon Haiku
   Journal*, v. 2

walking
from rain to sleet
to snow ...
the years sink deeper
into my bones

   ~Susan Constable, Never Ending Story, 2015

at eighty
he takes up the piano ...
practices
all the through the night
with two arthritic hands

   ~Susan Constable

the dance of flames
slowly reduced
to dying embers ...
their long-ago friendship
suddenly rekindled

   ~Susan Constable

maple leaves
in a dozen shades
of glory ...
so much beauty to be found
in the autumn of our lives

~Susan Constable

bus terminal----
an old man
savors his popcorn

~Julia Cousineau, in N. M. Sola, ed. *Four Hundred and Two Snails: HSA Members' Anthology, 2018*

winter moon —
are we done being lovers
old man

~Wanda D. Cook, *Modern Haiku*, 44.3, 2013

not one photo
of my childhood best friend
empty chrysalis

   ~ Wanda D. Cook, bottle rockets, #33, 2015

seinfeld reruns
after her stroke
all new episodes

   ~ Wanda D. Cook

anniversary celebration
their famous dance move
a medicare twirl

   ~ Wanda D. Cook

agreeing to make love
till they're ancient
— not tonight dear

   ~ Wanda D. Cook

toys ...
my father couldn't fix
summer rain

   ~ Aubrie Cox, Out of Translation, 2015

oak moon
all that's left of the crib
is splinters

   ~ Aubrie Cox, Out of Translation, 2015

black water bayou
whispering names
of old gods

    ~*Aubrie Cox, Out of Translation,* 2015

planting flowers
my father packs soil
with his cane

    ~*Kyle D. Craig, The Heron's Nest,* 19, 2017

~*Mary Davila*, 61st World Haiku Association Haiga Contest, 2008

suddenly seventy
I hear doors locking
as I pray
by myself in the first pew
...unnoticed

~*Mary Davila*

seems like yesterday
we went shopping for cribs
today we decide
above-ground or in-ground
for our final resting place

   ~*Mary Davila, Skylark* 6:1, 2018

I've come back
to this poem but can't figure out
what I was thinking…
the pause
in a hummingbird's flight

   ~*Mary Davila, Skylark* 5:1, 2017

ten years ago
I surrendered my keys…
it all came back today
driving around the store
in a handicapped cart

   ~*Mary Davila, Ribbons*, 12:2, 2016

middle age I believe the azaleas' pink lies

~Cherie Hunter Day, Frogpond, 36:1, 2013

along the drip line
of century old redwoods —
forget-me-nots

~Cherie Hunter Day, The Heron's Nest, 15, 2013

memorial park the December of soldiers' names

~Cherie Hunter Day, The Heron's Nest, 15, 2013

donating
my son's cello —
red leaves in the wind

~Cherie Hunter Day, Shiki List Kukai, 2009

birthday the white dahlia when I close my eyes

   ~ Cherie Hunter Day, Modern Haiku, 43.2, 2012

aging is so hard
on those who take care of
those who are

   ~ Marcyn Del Clemente

all her married life
she slept on the right side
now she takes center

   ~ Marcyn Del Clemente

This Too Too Fragile Veil

her hair falls
like golden ribbons down her back
mine falls out

hair brush
full of grey hair
am I

in the wrong house?
I'm a blond
What's gray hair

doing in my hairbrush?
why does my blond hair
turn gray

in the hairbrush?
arthritic hands
weave a braid

pink hair extension
she always forgets
to braid her hair BEFORE

inserting hearing aids
pigtails
and hearing aids

pigtails
and hearing aids
she's stylin'

that old woman
don't know who she is
in the mirror

    ~Marcyn Del Clemente

more and more lately
her scrapbook filled with obits

~*Marcyn Del Clemente*

all his paintings
his life's work on the walls
in this old house

~*Marcyn Del Clemente*

age happens
a bit of color still
in the dogwood

~*Ellen Compton, Modern Haiku*, 41.2, 2010

telling classmates
her hospitalized father
misplaced his hip

   ~ Robert Deluty, Momentary Blessings, 2019

the old man claiming
his little black book contains
mostly physicians

   ~ Robert Deluty, Momentary Blessings, 2019

pulling her
into sunlight
on my old sled

   ~ Charlotte Digregorio, Haiku & Senryu: A Simple Guide for All, 2014

forty-fifth reunion . . .
seniors
again

   ~ Charlotte Digregorio, Haiku & Senryu: A
   Simple Guide for All, 2014

aging . . .
getting the freckles
i wanted in childhood

   ~ Charlotte Digregorio, Haiku & Senryu: A
   Simple Guide for All, 2014

summer solstice . . .
warming my dying mother
with nonna's old blankets

   ~ Charlotte Digregorio, Haiku & Senryu: A
   Simple Guide for All, 2014

childless . . . .
looking at grandmother's face
in the mirror

   ~*Charlotte Digregorio, Haiku & Senryu: A Simple Guide for All,* 2014

storm aftermath
distant cry of an old man
searching for his dog

   ~*Karen DiNobile, Frogpond,* 42.1, 2019

still pond
the frog no longer
a tadpole

   ~*J Hahn Doleman*

middle age
discovering nothing
is wrinkle free

   ~J Hahn Doleman, Haibun Today, 13.1, 2019

grandma beating me again
. . . at hopscotch

   ~J Hahn Doleman

police chief
retiring from the force
. . . of gravity

   ~J Hahn Doleman

third wedding
she uncorks
the last Syrah

~J Hahn Doleman, *Modern Haiku*, 49.3, 2018

the old oak gone -
less and less of mum
remembering me

~*Steve Dolphy, Presence,* #61, 2018

our elderly neighbour
her curtains always open -
waiting to wave

~*Steve Dolphy*

the man who chose my name
no longer able
to write his own

   ~Steve Dolphy

September afternoon -
I read about ancestor worship
amongst toppled graves

   ~Stephen Dolphy, Blithe Spirit, 12:4, 2002

the last rose -
how long still
her perfume?

   ~Anna Maria Domburg-Sancristoforo

doves in autumn -
so far away my first kiss

~*Anna Maria Domburg-Sancristoforo*

autumn wind -
increasingly empty
my luggage

~*Anna Maria Domburg-Sancristoforo*

dusk -
what is done
is done

~*Anna Maria Domburg-Sancristoforo*

mom's
languished face
autumn leaf

    ~*Radostina Dragostinova, Autumn Moon Haiku Journal,* 2:1, *2018*

another birthday
in my mirror
a child smiling

    ~*Radostina Dragostinova, Bonsai,* 2, *2018*

dandelions meadow
is she still looking
for a donor

    ~*Radostina Dragostinova, Femku,* 3, *2018*

white crows
granny sending
postcards from heaven

   *~ Radostina Dragostinova, World Haiku
     Review,* 2018

autumn sea...
the driftwood shapes
of old grief

   ~ Rebecca Drouilhet, The Heron's Nest, 19, 2017

old moon the body my body remembers

   ~ Rebecca Drouilhet, Modern Haiku, 49.1, 2018

spring wind
my granddaughter's magic wand
makes me young

   ~Rebecca Drouilhet, *The Heron's Nest*, 18, 2016

nursing home
her only visitor
the therapy dog

   ~John J. Dunphy, *Akitsu Journal*, 2019

leaving the bar
I stumble on the doorstep —
first bifocals

   ~John J. Dunphy, *The Mid-America Poetry Review*, 5:2, 2004

Woodstock reunion
all the tie-dye shirts
XXX-large

~*John J. Dunphy, bottle rockets, #22, 2010*

aging puppeteer
his Punch and Judy
both trembling

~*John J. Dunphy, Modern Haiku, 23.2, 1992*

nursing home
beneath the old woman's pillow
a gold tooth

~*John J. Dunphy, Frogpond 19:1, 1996*

she shakes the wrinkles
from her square dance dresses
autumn colours

~Garry Eaton

these Christmas lights —
how I wish my children
were still small

~Lynn Edge, Chrysanthemum, 18, 2015

his yellow kayak
hangs from the rafters...
another year passing

~Lynn Edge, The Heron's Nest, 18, 2016

How quietly
the roses wither –
no screaming here

   ~Bruce England, Mu, #1, 2011

Family albums
remember the fifties
in black and white

   ~Bruce England, Frogpond, 43.1, 2018

Getting older
you begin to find out
how much you like
or dislike the DNA
of your ancestors

   ~Bruce England, in M. Kei, ed. Bright Stars: An Organic Tanka Anthology, #7, 2014

Unable to sleep
I step outside
see the morning star –
which regret greater
my lived or unlived life

~*Bruce England, A Hundred Gourds*, 3.1, 2013

Outside our window
blue sky, gulls flying
seemingly out to sea
the world baffles me
I don't want to leave yet

~*Bruce England, Atlas Poetica*, #24, 2016

long stem daisies
I return for a moment
to the summer of love

~*Robert Epstein, The Heron's Nest*, 15, 2013

I don't recall
ordering this
arthritis

   ~ Robert Epstein

in his poem
he once again sports
a full head of hair

   ~ Robert Epstein

a toothless cat
a blind dog
snuggling

   ~ Robert Epstein

slowly, slowly
all the way home
the old hiking couple

~Robert Epstein

forget-me-nots
the places her memory
no longer goes

~Kimberly Esser

another birthday
relighting
last year's candles

~Kimberly Esser, in B. Dee, ed. *Island of Egrets: Southern California Haiku Study Group Anthology*, 2010

first grey hair
polishing the mirror
a second time

   ~Kimberly Esser

being mistaken
for my mother
cold coffee

   ~Kimberly Esser

stitch by stitch
her life comes together
memory quilt

   ~Kimberly Esser, in Naia, ed. *What the Wind Can't Touch: Southern California Haiku Study Group Anthology,* 2016

following the grain...
grandfather's chisel
warms to his palm

~Claire Everett, The Heron's Nest, 19, 2017

her legs
in high heels
feeling my age

~Ignatius Fay

love poems
written in high school
naive
still they tighten
this aging throat

~Ignatius Fay

twenty-five years
since I last made love
imagine
quite the dry spell
I miss it...I think

~*Ignatius Fay*

my bladder
like the rest of me
getting older
more time needed
to get the job done

~*Ignatius Fay*

aging
that point in my life
it matters little
that the meal cools
or the iced tea warms

~*Ignatius Fay*

Orion's Belt
the globe spins
me again

   ~Bruce H. Feingold, Acorn, #38, 2017

sandstorm
an old man studies
bending palms

   ~Bruce H. Feingold, in M. Ahearn, ed. *Cherry Blossom Light: Yuki Tekei Haiku Society Members' Anthology,* 2016

waning crescent moon dad's pill cutter now mine

   ~Bruce H. Feingold, Modern Haiku, 50.1, 2019

old enough
to just listen
trout rising

~*Bruce H. Feingold, The Heron's Nest, #15 , 2013*

Milky Way
the last years of my life
the beginning of his

~*Bruce H. Feingold, Presence, #57, 2017*

two elderly women
at a table at the cafe
talking to one another
voice to voice, person to person
not using cell phones

~*Michael Fessler, Blithe Spirit, 25:2, 2015*

winter afternoon
so old that when I turn to look
I have to move
not just my neck but my entire
body—the whole jalopy

   ~Michael Fessler, *Also*, 2019

today I bought
one of those old man's hats
to keep the sun off
you can crumple it up
then crumple yourself up

   ~Michael Fessler, *Also*, 2019

RIP
my
tooth
passes
away

   ~Michael Fessler, *Also*, 2019

my present status:
I'm a haunted house
full of ghosts
but when you read my poems
you'll laugh at what scares me

~*Michael Fessler*, Also, 2019

so much love
dancing the parquet floor
on Sundays
when the jazz band plays
in the seniors' village

~*Amelia Fielden*

turned seventy
I see myself possibly
organising
my stamp collection
when I am old

~*Amelia Fielden*

my first lover
has Alzheimer's now
his wife says
he calls her by my name
on the beach of our past

~Amelia Fielden

when did he start
walking so slowly?
years and years
of fast strides, and now
"what's the rush" he complains

~Amelia Fielden

the fragrance
from white lilac subtler
than expected ...
letting go of the old age
I had imagined for us

~Amelia Fielden

old friend
knapsack intact
into the balsams

    ~*Madeleine Findlay, Empty Boathouse: Adirondack Haiku*, 2008

old logging road –
deer tracks and boot prints
intertwine

    ~*Madeleine Findlay, Empty Boathouse: Adirondack Haiku*, 2008

in her red beret
the old woman makes change –
U-Pick Apples

    ~*Madeleine Findlay, Under the Moon: Haiku & Senryu*, 2012

once a teenage crush
now it's the fresh drops of rain
on his rough tweed

    ~*Madeleine Findlay, Under the Moon: Haiku & Senryu*, 2012

antique show
a faded Amish bonnet
holds its shape

    ~*Madeleine Findlay, Under the Moon: Haiku & Senryu*, 2012

Still shining
over the old pond
light from a fallen star

    ~*Sylvia Forges-Ryan, What Light There is: Haiku, Senryu, and Tanka*, 2016

Spring cleaning
sorting toys in the attic
for my child's child

   ~ *Sylvia Forges-Ryan, What Light There is:*
   Haiku, Senryu, and Tanka, 2016

Meeting by chance
after so many years
I try to remember
what it was about you
I so much loved

   ~ *Sylvia Forges-Ryan, What Light There is:*
   Haiku, Senryu, and Tanka, 2016

To centuries-old ruins
you too must have seen
I whisper your name

   ~ *Sylvia Forges-Ryan, What Light There is:*
   Haiku, Senryu, and Tanka, 2016

A field of sunflowers
    all my summers
        clear back to childhood

  ~Sylvia Forges-Ryan, What Light There is:
  Haiku, Senryu, and Tanka, 2016

writing more
condolences than poems —
middle age

  ~Stanford M. Forrester

dinnertime —
the old cat regains
his hearing

  ~Stanford M. Forrester

more
snow
more

snow
my old
age

shaved
off
until

the
next
morning

~*Stanford M. Forrester*

after each haiku
the pencil
a little shorter

~*Stanford M. Forrester*

landing on
the hydrangea's last color
white butterfly

   ~*Stanford M. Forrester*

yozakura
two old lovers
renew their vows

   ~ *Terri L. French*, Vancouver Cherry Blossom Festival Haiku Contest, 2018; Honorable Mention

in the old maid's
flower box —
bachelor buttons

   ~*Terri L. French, haigaonline,* 2010

my eldest son's birthday
trying to recall
his little boy voice

~ *Terri L. French, Failed Haiku, #33, 2018*

the dawdle in
an autumn day
   old men in the park
debate Kant's views
   of space and time

~ *Terri L. French, dailyhaiga, 2013*

~ Terri French

smooth cemetery stone
I run my fingers
across her lifetime

   ~*Jay Friedenberg,* The Fifth Annual Peggy
     Willis Lyles Haiku Awards, 2017; Third Place

cicada husk
the mark from my wedding ring
already fading

   ~*Joshua Gage, Modern Haiku,* 48.1, 2017

judo master
confined to a wheel chair
...still has a move or two

   ~ *William Scott Galasso, Paper Wasp,* 21.3, 2015

a few precious steps...
the muscle memory
of dancehall days

   ~ William Scott Galasso, cattails, 2017

obituary...
the name of a woman
I loved as a girl

   ~ William Scott Galasso, Paper Wasp, 22.1, 2016

menopause
dueling
thermostats

   ~ William Scott Galasso, Failed Haiku, #24, 2017

oldies station
talkin' bout my
gggeneration

   ~ William Scott Galasso

younger brother
trying not to be
the older brother

   ~Mike Gallagher

Bing Crosby singing
White Christmas
the old man nodding

   ~Mike Gallagher

echoing
somewhere back then
a shepherd's call

   ~*Mike Gallagher*

old metronome—
where time
now rests

   ~*Michael J. Galko,* in N. M. Sola, ed. *Four Hundred and Two Snails: HSA Members' Anthology, 2018*

a fresh flush
of old man's beard
the path narrows

   ~*Tim Gardiner, The Mainichi Daily News, 2016*

morning sun
a retired greyhound
chases the breeze

   ~ Tim Gardiner

mimicking the cicada's language an old man's stick

   ~ Tim Gardiner

fading
on the yellowed calendar
ambitions

   ~ Marita Gargiulo

if only I didn't remember
the space race so vividly -
you, so vaguely

~ Marita Gargiulo

books in the attic
accepting
your goneness

~ Marita Gargiulo

pawnshop brass mouthpiece
a concerto from childhood
passes through my lips

~ Marita Gargiulo

grandma's old homestead
keeping with tradition
new immigrants settle in

~ *Marita Gargiulo*

Along the way
an old oak branch
becomes a walking stick

~ *Garry Gay, The Long Way Home,* 1999

ticks and tocks
the sounds of time...
old man foot taps
pcg '19

~ *Pat Geyer*

birthday outing...
a scenic ride
into my
golden years
gives me hope

~ *Pat Geyer*

gravity,
her birthday balloon hits
the ceiling...
seventy years old she counts
how many times it can bounce

~ *Pat Geyer*

sixty-seven
divided by two...
a magic age
when I was still playing
the newlywed game

~ *Pat Geyer*

counting the rings
in a ginkgo tree
goes on for days...
deep time passes
to the joshua tree

~Pat Geyer

blueberry pie
and a call from my sister
another birthday

~Merrill Ann Gonzales, Frogpond, 41:3, 2018

two old widows
caught in an ice storm
sharing rock salt

~Merrill Ann Gonzales, New England Letters, #93, 2019

a banyan tree
grows beyond
the elder's story

    ~*Brent Goodman, Frogpond,* 41.2, 2018

the good soldier
the ancestor who lived to tell
nothing

    ~*LeRoy Gorman, The Heron's Nest*, 19, 2017

married & gone
the last of her unicorns
dusty on a shelf

    ~*LeRoy Gorman, cattails,* 2018

waterfall
the streak of grey
in my wife's hair

> ~*Rob Grotke,* in N. M. Sola, ed. *Four Hundred and Two Snails: HSA Members' Anthology,* 2018

the big dipper
some childhood books
I can't part with

> ~*Carolyn Hall, bottle rockets,* #18, 2008

you *can* forget
how to ride a bike
   autumn leaves

> ~*Carolyn Hall,* San Francisco International Haiku Contest, 2011; First Place

my eighth decade
how the rains
rearrange the creek

   ~ Carolyn Hall, Mariposa, #34, 2016

less future than past —
an inchworm tests the void
beyond my fingertip

   ~ Carolyn Hall, The Heron's Nest, 19, 2017

a wish list
for my next life
autumn blaze maple

   ~ Carolyn Hall, Acorn, #35, 2015

squash vines
rambling everywhere
varicose veins

   ~Jennifer Hambrick

freezer burn
the stock boy
calls me *ma'am*

   ~Jennifer Hambrick

tree knots
the ancient wounds
that made the old gal tough

   ~Jennifer Hambrick

empty nest
they head out
for the early-bird special

~*Jennifer Hambrick*

an old man
learns two new words
cherry blossom

~*Jennifer Hambrick,* Vancouver Cherry Blossom Festival International Haiku Invitational, 2017; U. S. Sakura Award

senior poetry club
sharing grandkids' photos
before the session

~*John J. Han*

near retirement
three men discuss ways
to appease wives

~John J. Han

senior yuletide party
the gift of a notebook
that says, *go long*

~John J. Han

Shakespeare on the green
ye olde squirrel up and
down the tree

~John J. Han

a small bunch of hair
combing it carefully
oh so carefully

   ~John J. Han

retired
emphasis
on the second syllable

   ~Charles Harmon, Frogpond, 42:1, 2019

they said
it wouldn't last
80th anniversary

   ~Charles Harmon

worth more now
dead than alive
million buck life policy

~ *Charles Harmon*

libido abates
ego moderates
superego dominates

~ *Charles Harmon*

at sixty-three
sister gets her first passport
another grandchild

~ *Charles Harmon*

their ancient hum
to sunrise
honeybees

    ~*Michele L. Harvey, The Heron's Nest*, 19, 2017

old books...
dust that has settled
in me

    ~*Michele L. Harvey*

hot flash –
all the sudden emails
for viagra

    ~*Michele L. Harvey*

cold snap
that neighbor boy
calls me grandma

~MIchele L. Harvey

golden days
drinking them
to the last drop

~Michele L. Harvey

retirement   next day his caregiver

~Patricia Harvey

great morning
waking up
no colace today

~ Patricia Harvey

his best time now   holding her hand

~ Patricia Harvey

Generation Turning

pause on sandy slope
adult daughter takes my arm
steady together
I still feel her tiny hand
held in trust on this gold slope

~ Shasta Hatter

Grandson

blue shoes on brown trunk
arms around dangling branches
orange shirt in orange leaves
your father calls you away
I recall him in that tree

~*Shasta Hatter, Poetry Pacific,* 2018

Old Flame Returning

eighteen years have passed
an old man stands at my door
your smile melts the years
pulling me into your arms
where we are lovers once more

~*Shasta Hatter, Tanka Journal,* # 7, 2018

all the guilt
of losing touch
old catcher's mitt

   ~*John Hawk, Frogpond*, 41:3, 2018

old sandbox
the weeds
all grown up

   ~*John Hawk*, Robert Spiess Memorial Haiku
    Contest, 2018; Third Place

pressed flower
a memory I've forgotten
to remember

   ~*Tia Haynes, Frogpond*, 41:2, 2018

spring rain
refreshes a tired man...
a glass of wine

   ~David He

a chill wind
Granny shivers
white cones glisten

   ~David He

a skylark hovers
the old man seeding
morning glories

   ~David He

Christmas Eve
our faces brighten
by the pine tree
I remember
the box Dad gave me

   ~ David He

at the crossroads
we each pick a strand
from the weeping willow
to exchange when we part . . .
dew drops for the moment

   ~ David He

childhood's end
a carved-out pumpkin
and a conscience

   ~ Kyle Hemmings

wishing for a lover
i smooth the wrinkles
in my bed

   ~Kyle Hemmings

his childhood files :: the rats are not drawn to size

   ~Kyle Hemmings

black-hole moon
i'm still dying
from a childhood disease

   ~Kyle Hemmings, Human/Kind Journal, 1.1, 2019

stumps in the woods
    where old trees once stood
    a deeper stillness

~*Christopher Herold, Inside Out,* 2010

tea grown cold —
    the sleeping face
    of my old dog

~*Christopher Herold, Inside Out,* 2010

bored by my yoga
the old cat closes his eyes
and licks his loins

~*Christopher Herold, Inside Out,* 2010

cottonwood seeds
   three old men doing tai chi
      by the river

  ~Christopher Herold, Inside Out, 2010

spring morning
the art of walking beside
someone much older

  ~Christopher Herold, Inside Out, 2010

Navajo Land

cliff dwellings
from a crumbling wall
a crow watches us

morning birdsong
the old woman weaves it
into her blanket

search for arrowheads
beside an ant hill
a shark's tooth

Monument Valley
a hawk's slow circle
a sonic boom

lazy buzzard
waiting for the sun
to do its job

a dozen iphones
snap photos of petroglyphs
signed by a handprint

planting corn
the old man sings
to each seed

~*Frank Higgins, Frogpond,* 41:3, 2018

pies cooling
a child teaches gramma
her vowels

   ~*Frank Higgins*

high blood pressure
my father's son
after all

   ~*Frank Higgins*

old beachcombers
   she holds the shell
   to his good ear

~ Frank Higgins

a boy watching
his father shave
his father

~ Frank Higgins

old dreams revealed
Elvis at the senior center

~ Judith Hishikawa, in N. M. Sola, ed. *Four Hundred and Two Snails: HSA Members' Anthology,* 2018

trying to accommodate
one body part,
the others complain

   ~*Judith Hishikawa*

rooted in time
the historical society
librarian

   ~*Judith Hishikawa*

retired school teacher
still pulling red pens
out of her purse

   ~*Judith Hishikawa, bottle rockets,* #35, 2016

gnarled oak
still dropping
acorns

~*Judith Hishikawa*

reunion night
my old teakwood bed
cranky and grouchy

~*Su Wai Hlaing Failed Haiku*, #37, 2019

dandelion clock
am I running out of time?

~*Su Wai Hlaing*

his wrinkled hands
hunting for cigarettes
unfinished

~ *Su Wai Hlaing*

again, today
Dad is looking for
house keys

~ *Su Wai Hlaing*

unpacking
the old house
in the new place

~ *Su Wai Hlaing*

in time
our starter home becomes
our final one

   ~Ruth Holzer

slowing
my pace
to his—
I recall my first two-wheeler
released from guiding hands

   ~Ruth Holzer

born bald
bald again—
a late birthday

   ~Ruth Holzer

tai chi class—
the ladies
with titanium knees

~ Ruth Holzer

standing
on the threshold
Mother sighs
*I really don't like
this stage of life*

~ Ruth Holzer

outlasting Mom
pairs of shoes
on the closet floor

~ Gary Hotham, *The Heron's Nest,* 19, 2017

spring cleaning...
mother's lost Christmas money
behind an old photograph

   ~ *Elizabeth Howard, Frogpond*, 42:1, 2019

delete, delete
delete
senior moments

   ~ *Terrie Jacks, Failed Haiku*, #20, 2017

autumn
a scarecrow in the field
slumps exhausted

   ~ *Terrie Jacks, Failed Haiku*, #34, 2018

birch limbs –
long thin fingers
of an ancient hand,
wrinkled and pale,
lured by the sun

~ *Terrie Jacks, cattails, 2017*

her birthday
– afraid to measure
in dog years

~ *Roberta Beach Jacobson*

again?
an invitation to
the class reunion

~ *Roberta Beach Jacobson*

carrying
my old union card
long after retirement

   ~ Roberta Beach Jacobson

stealing his
retirement dreams
– dementia

   ~ Roberta Beach Jacobson

the teen grabs maps
from my glove box
asking "Is this an atlas?"

   ~ Roberta Beach Jacobson

in my ninth decade
enjoying everything saved
for special occasions

   ~ Gloria Jaguden

ninth decade
the lines in my palm
disappear

   ~ Gloria Jaguden

death date
his old jacket
keeps me warm

   ~ Gloria Jaguden

these summer mornings
I would do everything
even the bad stuff again

   ~ Gloria Jaguden

aging in place
another step
without falling

   ~ Peter Jastermsky

senior center
finding my father's
favorite chair

   ~ Peter Jastermsky

old songs
a wrinkle disappears
with each line

~*Peter Jastermsky*

unchained memory
another burnt pot
of vegetables

~*Peter Jastermsky*

resting where
the commas fall –
old friends

~*Peter Jastermsky*

searching through pennies my old thoughts

~ *PMF Johnson, Frogpond,* 41:2, 2018

playground half
the size I remember–
scattered leaves

~ *PMF Johnson, The Heron's Nest,* 19, 2017

in the desk drawer
the yellowed ticket
to visit you in Paris

~ *Frank Judge, Frogpond,* 41:2, 2018

the falling dark
and the becoming light
old age

~ *Jim Kacian*

death of an old flame a hard nostalgia

~ *Jim Kacian*

pilgrimage to a certain tree childhood

~ *Jim Kacian*

for
getting
me
mories

~ Jim Kacian

spring wind
the scent
of other springs

~ Jim Kacian

for a long time after
what the tree remembers
of the rain

   ~Elmedin Kadric, buying time, 2017

burning bush
what to become
when I'm old

   ~Elmedin Kadric, buying time, 2017

moth night growing old in the light

   ~Elmedin Kadric

deciduous
what her legs
used to be

   ~ Elmedin Kadric

Father's Day
the conversation returns
to the old days

   ~ Elmedin Kadric

fingernail moon
letting them glimpse
my inner crone

   ~ Barbara Kaufmann, tinywords, 2018

a long ago promise
threaded with the gold of autumn
we hold
the warm sunlight
each for the other

   ~Barbara Kaufmann, in M. Dornhous and D. Terelink, eds. *The Right Touch of Sun: The Tanka Society Members' Anthology*, 2017

a basket of notebooks
filled to the brim
with poems
how can my old heart
hold them all

   ~Barbara Kaufmann, Frameless Sky, 2014

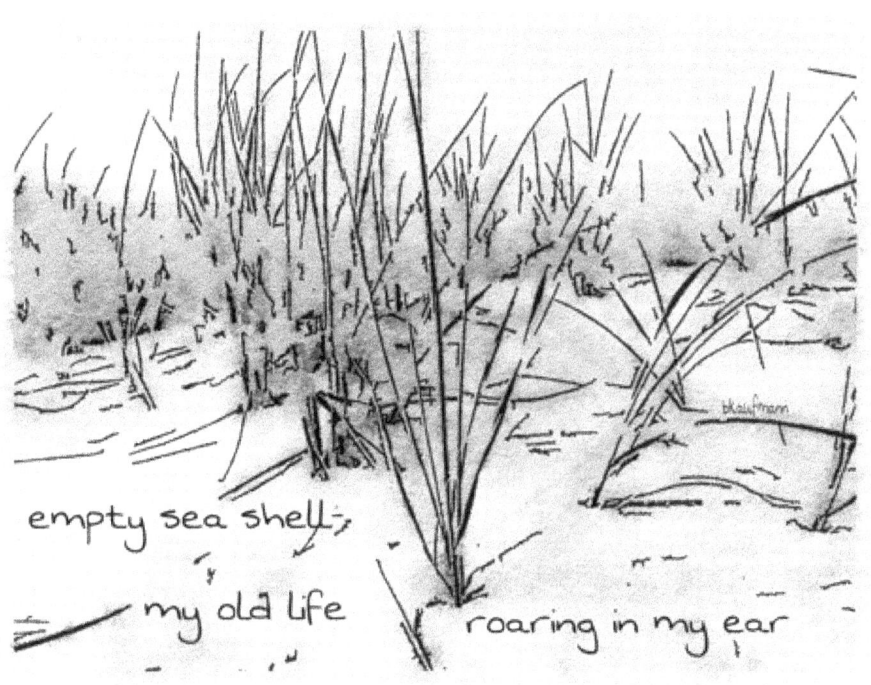

~ Barbara Kaufmann

the birds and the bees
how my body remembers
early spring

~ Barbara Kaufmann

~ Mary Kendall, Tom Claussen (Art),
www.dailyhaiga.org, 2015

the house
where I was born
weeds & more weeds

~*Mary Kendall, Prune Juice, #26, 2018*

scent of mock orange –
all the years spent
doubting myself

~*Mary Kendall, brass bell,* 2017

Queen Anne's lace—
a childhood spent
in second hand clothes

~*Mary Kendall, The Heron's Nest,* 19, 2017; Editors' Choices

almost toothless
the old dog sleeps
by the fire. . .
the peace of knowing
you are there

> ~ *Mary Kendall,* in S. Krishnamurthy, ed.
> *Of Love and War: Tanka Society of America Members' Anthology,* 2018

summer night...
too old for flirting
we do it anyway

> ~ *Bill Kenney, Modern Haiku,* 47.1, 2016

parts
   of the river
the river
   leaves behind

> ~ *Brendon Kent, Wales Haiku Journal, 2018;*
> *for Krish*

flickering
around the campfire
childhood

   ~ Brendon Kent, in J. Salzer & the Nook Editorial Staff, eds., *Yanty's Butterfly: Haiku Nook: An Anthology*, 2016

homo naledi
in these old bones
the weight
of all we know
and all we don't

   ~ Brendon Kent, hedgerow, #14, 2017

every step
to the bathroom light
aging moon

   ~ Brendon Kent

obituary...
catching up
on old friends

   ~Brendon Kent

admiring the pipes
at the headshop counter
grey beard guy and green hair guy

   ~Michael Ketchek, *Haiku for Hippies*, 2000

resting in the shade
my old backpack
also shows the miles

   ~Michael Ketchek, *Black Bough*, 5, 1995

her old love beads
found in the attic, hesitantly
she tries them on

 ~Michael Ketchek, *Haiku for Hippies,* 2000

grandpa chuckling
double parked by the clinic
again no ticket

 ~Michael Ketchek, *Frogpond,* 14:4, 1991

snow covered ground
no one remembers me
as a baby

 ~Michael Ketchek, *Who I Am,* 2015

growing
with the mango tree
my grandfather planted

   ~ Mohammad Azim Khan

ageing rosewood
the envy
of the forest

   ~ Mohammad Azim Khan

shrinking sun ...
two old men
on the chessboard

   ~ Mohammad Azim Khan

last chapter
of my life ...
physicians and surgeons

   ~Mohammad Azim Khan

your face
is my fortune –
together
we move towards
the full glow

   ~Mohammad Azim Khan

all gone
God, angels, heaven, gold crown
the taste of water

   ~Howard Lee Kilby

the fear of old age
has long since fallen away
I sing a new song

   ~ Howard Lee Kilby

as the water skier lets go
     slows &
          sinks, so
this epilogue
to a bookman's long career

   ~ Larry Kimmel, Skylark, 3:1, 2015

while I slept
it snowed
and a tree fell
old age
uncertain as a winter road

   ~ Larry Kimmel, Tanka Journal, #23, 2003

the gnarled apple tree in winter
now lush with leaves —
the twists
and turns of growth —
my own strange armature

~*Larry Kimmel, World Haiku Review*, 2005

she is not so deaf
the neighbor's relentless dog
is lost to her
but the crickets
where did the crickets go?

~*Larry Kimmel, Eucalypt*, #2, 2007

the river snakes
across the plain into
the blue distance —
it's not so much a fear of what's to come
as of nothing left to do

~*Larry Kimmel, still* 5 *two*, 2001

faded ribbon
the stiff keys of old
typewriters

   ~*Deborah P. Kolodji, San Diego Poetry Annual,*
   2016-2017

lock of baby hair
from his first haircut–
my dreams for him

   ~*Deborah P. Kolodji, Mainichi Daily News,*
   2007

horse calendar
Grandmother dreams
she's bareback

   ~*Deborah P. Kolodji, Rattle,* 2015

last jar
of apricot
jam
her old apron

   ~Deborah P. Kolodji, Riverbed Haiku, 2008

rings
   of old trees the slowness
             of footsteps

   ~Paul Kulwatno

the mirror
   a face richer
      with furrows

   ~Paul Kulwatno

mid-fifties
   she understands physics
                at last

~*Paul Kulwatno*

~*Lavana Kray, www.dailyhaiga.org*, 2017

childhood locked
behind the dollhouse door –
the garage sale

> ~*Natalia Kuznetsova, World Haiku Review*, 2018; Haiku of Merit

the waning moon
captured in the disused well...
old-age seclusion

> ~*Natalia Kuznetsova, World Haiku Review*, 2018; Haiku of Merit

autumn sun
the old oak's shadow
unwanted

> ~*Natalia Kuznetsova, Asahi Haikuist Network*, 2015

retirement –
turning the final page
in this suspense book

    ~Natalia Kuznetsova, Asahi Haikuist Network,
    2018

silver jubilee –
the cherry planted that day
blossoming anew

    ~Natalia Kuznetsova, World Haiku Review,
    2015; Honorable Mention

little Bessie
four years old
plus ninety

    ~David G. Lanoue

she's old
but at the piano
thunder!

   ~David G. Lanoue

Easter Sunday
grandpa puts on grandma's
wig

   ~David G. Lanoue

the old couple
eating dandelions
daintily

   ~David G. Lanoue

end of winter
a letter from the friend
I thought I'd lost

   ~*Catherine J.S. Lee, New England Letters*,
   #93, 2019

rainy season
the doctor assures me
it comes with age

   ~*Michael Henry Lee, cattails*, 2018

Indian summer
this month's featured reader at
the senior center

   ~*Michael Henry Lee*

jisei
the test of time on
a marble marker

   ~ *Michael Henry Lee*

over 55
putting the recliner
in reverse

   ~ *Brenda Lempp,* in N. M. Sola, ed. *Four Hundred and Two Snails: HSA Members' Anthology,* 2018

like my trips
several times each night
to the loo
the old years come and go
with increasing urgency

   ~ *Michael Lester*

he has become
quite cantankerous
in his old age
but the grandchildren
would never know it

   ~Michael Lester

all these chips
in our old wedding dishes—
no matter
how careful we are
someone always gets hurt

   ~Michael Lester

older now
but none the wiser
I refuse
to wear hearing aids
or senior diapers

   ~Michael Lester

together
we enjoy the stillness
and warmth
of a country evening
on our old porch swing

~*Michael Lester*

The old oak table
where the photograph once stood –
a bowl of apples

~*Priscilla Lignori*

At the polling place
reaching into my purse to
find my new glasses

~*Priscilla Lignori, Eastern Structures, #2, 2016*

on a bicycle
learning to balance again –
sixty-three years young

    ~ Priscilla Lignori, World Haiku Review, 2017

Two inches wider
quarter of an inch shorter –
trying on swimsuits

    ~ Priscilla Lignori

a certain calling
draws me deep into the woods –
ancestor voices

    ~ Priscilla Lignori, Asahi Haikuist Network, 2017

Distant thunder . . .
skeletons of old cars
dim in the junkyard

   ~Rebecca Lilly, Shadwell Hills, 2002

Goats grazing weeds
around the maple stump –
my nostalgia deepens

   ~Rebecca Lilly, Yesterday's Footprints, 2012

Lulled by a moth
fluttering in pulled curtains . . .
his boyhood home

   ~Rebecca Lilly, Yesterday's Footprints, 2012

Other reminiscences
follow this one . . .
grasses' yellow tints

   ˜*Rebecca Lilly, Yesterday's Footprints,* 2012

The old well:
rain falling
into its echoes . . .

   ˜*Rebecca Lilly, Yesterday's Footprints,* 2012

first snow flurries. . .
the shape of the day
after retirement

   ˜*Chen-ou Liu, The Heron's Nest,* 15, 2013

closed daisies
my layers
of gray

~ *Cyndi Lloyd, Modern Haiku,* 50.1, 2019

the butterfly
slips from the chrysalis
how soft my skin used to be

~ *Cyndi Lloyd*, Shiki Monthly Kukai, 2015

children leave...
the distant mountains
even farther away

~ *Cyndi Lloyd*, European Quarterly Kukai, #13, 2016

snowflakes stick
to the dog's back –
the weight of aging

   ~ *Cyndi Lloyd, Frogpond*, 39:1, 2016

my remaining chips
on the blackjack table
70th birthday

   ~ *Gregory Longenecker*

I look around
for an old friend
Vietnam Wall

   ~ *Gregory Longenecker*

lingering heat
guitar riffs from
my neighbor's past

   ~Gregory Longenecker, Acorn, #39, 2017

moving day
we take apart the bed
our parents dreamed on

   ~Gregory Longenecker, H. Gene Murtha
   Senryu Contest 2017; First Place

senior center
I search for the man
he used to be

   ~Gregory Longenecker, in Naia, ed. *What the*
   Wind Can't Touch: Southern California
   Haiku Study Group Anthology, 2016

second childhood …
the old man teaches his aide
some words of Polish

~*Amy Losak*

music therapy
the old man with dementia
knows all the words

~*Amy Losak*

thin ice
an elderly couple
with their arms linked

~*Amy Losak*

peeling tree bark —
she hides her spotted hands
in the interview

   ~*Amy Losak*

waning sunset ...
who will care for me
when I get old?

   ~*Amy Losak*

summer evening
on an old Victrola
a scratchy ragtime tune

   ~*Patricia J. Machmiller, Frogpond,* 41:3, 2018

old year passing
Auld Lang Syne
on an untuned piano

   ~pjm (Patricia J. Machmiller), *Acorn,* #42, 2019

the spider, too
has survived another winter —
on a silk thread
it glides into sunlight
to spar with its shadow

   ~Carole MacRury, *Gusts*, 21, 2015

grapevines
weave their way through
a chain-link —
two enemies, grown old
decide to make wine

   ~Carole MacRury, *Gusts*, 28, 2018

she brings me
a bouquet of white roses
on my 70th—
how to speak to a daughter
of long-lost innocence

   ~*Carole MacRury, Gusts,* 21, 2015

as it was
in the beginning . . .
I, too
embrace all of these
maid, mother, crone

   ~*Carole MacRury, Gusts,* 20, 2014; 10th
    Anniversary Edition

sunlight
fills the emptiness
of a blue bowl—
this life of loving,
losing, letting go

~ *Carole MacRury,* in M. Dornhaus and D. Terelinck, eds. *The Right Touch of Sun: The Tanka Society of America Members' Anthology,* 2017

melting ice
her first letter after
fifty years

~ *Martha Magenta, brass bell,* 2017

driftwood the art of ageing

~ *Martha Magenta*

my dog years running wild with the moon

~*Martha Magenta*

her trips
to the botox clinic
autumn leaves

~*Martha Magenta, #FemkuMag, #6, 2018*

menopause
I save an egg
for my rebirth

~*Martha Magenta, #FemkuMag, #3, 2018*

a new stage of life –
the teenager gives his marbles
to his little brother

   ~ Tomislav Maretić

my old favorite pub –
younger and younger
visitors at bar

   ~ Tomislav Maretić

my childhood courtyard –
after so many deaths,
the old lilac in bloom

   ~ Tomislav Maretić

parchment
the poetry
of old oaks

~*Anna Maris and Chris Maris (art), www.dailyhaiga.org*, 2017

old linden tree before me and after

~*Anna Maris, Acorn,* #40, 2018

harvest festival
my shadow on the wall
still a young woman

~*Anna Maris*, 6th Polish International Haiku Competition; 2nd prize, 2016

autumn rain
aches and pains long forgotten
return

~*Anna Maris, Taj Mahal Review*, 2015

summers day
a dad shows his son
grandpa's work

~*Anna Maris, Daily Haiku*, cycle 20, 2016

lasts even longer
   faded
      cherry blossom

~*Jeannie Martin*

aging lover
we hold hands
on the icy path

   ~Jeannie Martin

retirement home
wondering about the age
of the giant pines

   ~Jeannie Martin

lace-leaf maples
aging too —
winter rain

   ~Jeannie Martin

waiting for spring
all the empty
nests

   ~Jeannie Martin

old
now
nothing

to be
done
taking

pliers
to my
glasses

   ~john martone, dogwood & honeysuckle, 2004

weathered
straw-

broom
out back

by
herb pots

    ~*john martone, dogwood & honeysuckle,* 2004

a
long
ago

baby
food
jar

for
bamboo cuttings

    ~*john martone, dogwood & honeysuckle,* 2004

my
aging
face

more
& more
mother

    ~john martone, dogwood & honeysuckle, 2004

sticks
of old

furni
ture
this book

    ~john martone, dogwood & honeysuckle, 2004

I want to be
like old wood, weathering
in sun, wind and rain —
a fence, a shack
a hut, a gate

~Joy McCall

a small chicken
pecks round the yard
dust on her feet
she is past laying eggs
yet how lovely her red feathers!

~Joy McCall

my maiden aunt
almost one hundred and three
lays in her bed
all day, all night
smiling, sleeping, smiling

~Joy McCall

I love old things
chairs, tables, floors
shovels, spades
worn and faded things
telling their long stories

   ~Joy McCall

old love
that has stood
the test of time
is solid ground
beneath my feet

   ~Joy McCall

an old reed song
my boat drifts
in that direction

   ~ Michael McClintock, The Heron's Nest,
     15, 2013

morning fog. . .
when my embryo
had gills

~ *Tyrone McDonald, The Heron's Nest,*
15, 2013

each day the wind
takes a little more of me
late afternoon shadow

~ *Marietta McGregor, Under the Basho, 2018*

~ Marietta McGregor, *Under the Basho*, 2018

settling fog
grandpa surrenders
his car license

~*Marietta McGregor, Failed Haiku, #33*, 2018

knowing now
what we couldn't know then
forsythia buds

~*Marietta McGregor, hedgerow, #67*, 2016

seventy-plus...
switching to
Jupiter years

~*Marietta McGregor, Failed Haiku, #6*, 2016

antique shop
everything older
than I am

> ~*Dorothy McLaughlin,* in N. M. Sola, ed. *Four Hundred and Two Snails: HSA Members' Anthology,* 2018

old comic books
my son meets the boy
I used to be

> ~*John McManus, The Heron's Nest*, 18, 2016

tin ceiling
grandma talks of a world
before the war

> ~*Ben Moeller-Gaa, Blithe Spirit*, 28:3, 2018

grandpa's silence
an enemy helmet behind
the attic door

   ~*Ben Moeller-Gaa, Chrysanthemum, #23, 2018*

her touch
after all these years —
Bach's piano

   ~*Ben Moeller-Gaa, cattails, 2018*

spring wind
spinning the barstool
the kid in me

   ~*Ben Moeller-Gaa, Under the Basho, 2017*

from the stump
of the old cherry tree
another cherry tree

   ~Ben Moeller-Gaa, Acorn, #32, 2014

at 70 mph changing leaves

   ~Matthew Moffett, Modern Haiku, 48.1, 2017

cold drizzle
preparing her
advance directive

   ~Beverly Acuff Momoi, Modern Haiku, 50.1, 2019

wasting moon
not seeing
the dropped stitches

> ~*Beverly Acuff Momoi, Modern Haiku,* 49.1, 2018

all the paths I didn't choose the Milky Way

> ~*Beverly Acuff Momoi, hedgerow,* #124, 2018

tipping his hat
to a young woman
his bald spot

> ~*Mike Montreuil*

is it old age
this urge
to pray again?

   ~*Mike Montreuil*

coffee going cold
my time here
almost over

   ~*Mike Montreuil*

were they
really like that?
endless summers

   ~*Mike Montreuil*

hundred-year-old oak
fallen from the hurricane —
clothesline still stands

   ~Lenard D. Moore, Frogpond, 42:1, 2019

sixtieth summer —
I fold the dryer's heat
into the towel

   ~Lenard D. Moore, Modern Haiku, 50.1, 2019

who hears . . .
the white of snow

who sees . . .
the sound of frogs

who knows . . .
the taste of stardust

~ *Ron Moss*

crescent moon
a bone carver sings
to his ancestors

   ~Ron C. Moss, *The Bone Carver*, 2014

old pine
drops its seed
on freshly cut grass

   ~Ron C. Moss, *The Bone Carver*, 2014

starry night
what's left of my life
is enough

   ~Ron C. Moss, *The Bone Carver*, 2014

not where
I left it
my childhood

    ~*Peter Newton, Modern Haiku, 49.2, 2018*

headlong of the jetty
    when I was
a superhero

    ~*Peter Newton, The Heron's Nest, 18, 2016*

old enough
now the willow sings
me to sleep

    ~*Peter Newton, The Heron's Nest, 19, 2017*

old friends –
longer phone calls
with fewer left

~ *Suzanne Niedzielska*

fear of falling
from downhill to cross-country —
skis to snowshoes

~ *Suzanne Niedzielska*

kitchen gadgets
mother forgets the names
of her daughters

~ *Nika,* in N. M. Sola, ed. *Four Hundred and Two Snails: HSA Members' Anthology,* 2018

does she know the address?
he did not ask me
as i have a cane

~ *Barbro Nilsson*

radio playing
the music feet remember
dancing the years away

~ *Barbro Nilsson*

still it is possible
to go skiing
in ones sleep

~ *Barbro Nilsson*

70th birthday
all the bills
are paid

   ~Patricia Nolan, Western Brushstrokes, 2009

grandchild's laughter
a taste of sunshine
for elders

   ~Patricia Nolan

baby teeth – old teeth
the tooth fairy only pays
young ones

   ~Patricia Nolan

re-reading
all the old books I've saved
for old age

~ *Patricia Nolan*

only took seven decades
to grow pretty hair
and maybe wisdom

~ *Patricia Nolan*

first age spots...
her hand even
more beautiful

~ *Réka Nyitrai, #FemKuMag, #2, 2018*

soon forty-one...
inside my head the cicadas
are singing about autumn

   ~ Réka Nyitrai, #FemKuMag, #4, 2018

first day of autumn —
watching mother's traits
take over my face

   ~ Réka Nyitrai, Failed Haiku, #33, 2018

twilight does the twig remember the pull of the leaf

   ~ Réka Nyitrai, Otata, #36, 2018

an old man
whistling a folk song —
winter begins

   ~*Réka Nyitrai, Failed Haiku*, #36, 2018

heat lightning
something ancient
in a lizard's eye

   ~*Polona Oblak, The Heron's Nest*, 19, 2017

clouds ride with me...
   dad's second stroke

   ~*Karen O' Leary,* in N. M. Sola, ed. *Four Hundred and Two Snails: HSA Members' Anthology*, 2018

sepia pages
peace settles
between the wrinkles

   ~Karen O' Leary, Sketchbook, 2011

memories of grandma...
mason jars of dandelion wine
on wood basement shelves

   ~Karen O' Leary

celebrating
60 years of marriage
chips and dip

   ~Karen O' Leary,
   www.peggyduganfrench.com/2018/05/
   Home of Shemom, 2018

years playing hearts…
my nephew teaches me
to shoot the moon

   ~Karen O' Leary

not yet written
in the overflowing book
cards and envelopes
with last known
addresses

   ~Ellen Grace Olinger,
     www.ellinolinger.wordpress.com, 2017

still wanting to remember
what may no longer
be current – places I was
people I knew

   ~Ellen Grace Olinger,
     www.ellinolinger.wordpress.com, 2017

roses in the sun
some ending
some beginning
and some in full bloom
good to grow older

   ~Ellen Grace Olinger,
     www.ellenolinger.wordpress.com, 2012

older now
used books settle
in their new home

   ~Ellen Grace Olinger,
     www.ellenolinger.wordpress.com, 2014

reading memoirs
and then the view
outside today

   ~Ellen Grace Olinger,
     www.ellenolinger.wordpress.com, 2015

vintage kimono
my seams unraveling
this perfect life

   ~ Renée Owen, Alone on a Wild Coast, 2014

sari silk scraps feeling a tug from my past life

   ~ Renée Owen, Alone on a Wild Coast, 2014

the fullness of time
my arm
around his waist

   ~ Lorraine A. Padden

we softly fall
from motherly jaws
once held tight

~*Lorraine A. Padden*

I spend time
as if it's not
my life passing

~*Lorraine A. Padden*

newborn—
grandfather reminisces
his mother

~*Pravat Kumar Padhy*

end of summer
an antique table fan
pauses for a while

   ~ Pravat Kumar Padhy

one year old kid—
lifting up rocks
a million years old

   ~ Pravat Kumar Padhy

cicada shell
our ten-year old says
he'll never leave home

   ~ Tom Painting, First Annual Peggy Willis
     Lyles Haiku Award; 4th Honorable Mention

magpie treasures—
dining hall salt shakers
fill grandma's purse

~*Carol Ann Palomba, hedgerow*, #69, 2016

twilight
waiting for an old dog
to find his way home

~*Carol Ann Palomba, Prune Juice*, #20, 2016

antiques
for our anniversary
a pair of red oars

~*Carol Ann Palomba, Frogpond*, 41:1, 2018

dawning autumn
I slip to the wrong side
of forties

   ~ *Vandana Parashar, Haiku Universe*, 2018

adulthood
how beautiful the world was
from a treehouse window

   ~ *Vandana Parashar, Scryptic Magazine*, 1.4, 2018

school reunion
no one recognises me
except the dog

   ~ *Vandana Parashar, Failed Haiku*, #35, 2018

party animal
I now watch cartoons
with my kids

~ *Vandana Parashar, Sonic Boom, 2015*

buying sneakers
he's trying his male voice
...early spring

~ *Kerstin Park*

magnolia blossoms
     your old sun hat is better
my daughter says

~ *Kerstin Park*

the pine's birthplace
beside the playground
my first love's name

~ Kerstin Park

mammography letter
i'm weeding the roses
first

~ Kerstin Park

window shopping
a wrinkled woman
turns up

~ Kerstin Park

old diary
the rose
still red

   ~Aparna Pathak, brass bell, 2017

wheeling her chair
through leaf fall. . .
we sure knew how to dance

   ~Bill Pauly, *The Heron's Nest*, 18, 2016;
   Editors' Choice

deep snow
I turn the pages
of an old passport

   ~Dru Philippou, *The Heron's Nest*, 15, 2013

a week at the beach
she learns again
to be a child

    ~*Gregory Piko, Paper Wasp*, 13:1, 2007

second honeymoon
a young couple's passion
in the room above

    ~*Gregory Piko, Paper Wasp*, 20:3, 2014

deaf as a post
I teach an old dog
sign language

    ~*Gregory Piko, Paper Wasp*, 19:3, 2013

pleased to find
she's doing so well
googling old loves

   ~*Gregory Piko, Paper Wasp*, 16:2, 2010

if someone asks
say I'm still writing . . .
the narrowing road

   ~*Gregory Piko, Modern Haiku*, 41.1, 2010

my coffee cup
shows New York City
with the Old World Trade Center

   ~*Jonathan Vost Post*

spent 77 years
not speaking a word
yucca

   ~*Jonathan Vos Post*

silence deepens
words no longer
on the tip of her tongue

   ~*Marilyn Powell, Akitsu Quarterly*, 2018

family reunion
he longs
for closed captioning

   ~*Marilyn Powell,* in N. M. Sola, ed. *Four Hundred and Two Snails: HSA Members' Anthology*, 2018

aging . . .
more men compliment
my dog

   ~Joan Prefontaine, bottle rockets, #33, 2015

a birthday card
compares me
to a fine aged wine
yet I feel more like
new vinegar

   ~Joan Prefontaine

we keep telling him
he's just a pup
our dog's 12th birthday

   ~Joan Prefontaine

competition
long after high school . . .
comparing grandkids

~*Joan Prefontaine*

called a cougar
for marrying
a younger man
uncertain whether
to growl or purr

~*Joan Prefontaine*

eightieth birthday –
he insists that we
aren't married

~*Geethanjali Rajan*

incontinence . . .
remains of rain
from the red-tile roof

   ~Geethanjali Rajan, The Third H. Gene Murtha Memorial Senryu Contest, 2018; Honorable Mention

seniors' home
grandma enquires about
her button roses

   ~Geethanjali Rajan, Brown Boat, 2014

she holds my hand
a little tighter
recollecting the past
as if I too
would slip away

   ~Geethanjali Rajan, Gogyoshi Monthly, 2015

summer's end
asking grandpa
if his wrinkles hurt

~*Carol Raisfield*

early to bed –
my arthritis, his bad back
young lovers in disguise

~*Carol Raisfield*

feet in stirrups –
the new gynecologist
her old paperboy

   ~ Carol Raisfield

sparking memories
I talk about the children
in the quiet
touching your cheek's curve
you don't know my name

   ~ Carol Raisfield

my daughter
looking both ways
takes my hand
the cane on my arm
I remember her pigtails

   ~ Carol Raisfield

   in mid-life
ripping out a boxwood
   of forty years

   ~ *William M. Ramsey, more wine,* 2010

slave cemetery
I scrape the moss to find
no name

   ~ *William M. Ramsey, this wine,* 2002

   pulling gate nails
driven by
   my young father

   ~ *William M. Ramsey, this wine,* 2002

my aging face
in the mirror softens
farsightedness

   ~*Nancy Rapp*

the walker
a new part
of my old dad

   ~*Nancy Rapp*

midwinter
the wight of my bones
on the hardwood floor

   ~*Nancy Rapp, Akitsu Quarterly*, 2018

icy wind . . .
the old post and rail
speckled with lichen

    ~*Lyn Reeves, Echidna Tracks: Australian Haiku, #2;* Landscapes, 2018

junk shop . . .
cobwebs curtain
the dollhouse windows

    ~*Lyn Reeves,* The Haiku Foundation; Windows, 2018

afternoon light
grandfather dances
in a shower of leaves

    ~*Lyn Reeves*

that distant ridge
I'll never climb . . .
autumn rain

   ~Lyn Reeves, Yellow Moon, 19, 2006

old town rivulet
its banks overrun
with forget-me-nots

   ~Lyn Reeves, Australian Haiku Society
   Summer Solstice String, 2018

withered
with
age
her
rose
tattoo

   ~Bryan Rickert, Prune Juice, #21, 2017

undressing
a glimpse of the girl
she used to be

    ~*Bryan Rickert, Prune Juice, #21, 2017*

church gossip
old women knitting
their brows

    ~*Bryan Rickert*

prairie lands
old thoroughbreds
jockey for carrots

    ~*Bryan Rickert*

senior living in the moment

~Bryan Rickert

retirement party
granddaughter's drawing,
she says, of her and me

~Edward J. Rielly

flower seeds drying
over winter . . .
our golden anniversary

~Edward J. Rielly

my sister's wake—
old friends
so much older

~*Edward J. Rielly*

adding prunes
to his cereal . . .
aged wisdom

~*Edward J. Rielly*

autumn leaves
old broom losing itself
bristle by bristle

~*Edward J. Rielly, The Heron's Nest,* 18, 2016

lopsided and wrinkled
the elder
handy with a pen

    ~Joan Marie Roberts

word games
exercise grey matter
too late

    ~Joan Marie Roberts

in the third stage of life
wisdom
no guarantee

    ~Joan Marie Roberts

lost in the woods
   the woods
      of my childhood

   ~*Chad Lee Robinson, The Heron's Nest, 15, 2015*

   ~*Chad Lee Robinson, The Heron's Nest*, 15, 2013

liver spots . . .
how lightly she holds
the tiger lily

   ~*Chad Lee Robinson, The Deep End of the Sky*, 2015

winter stars . . .
the name of my father
of my father's father

   ~*Chad Lee Robinson, The Deep End of the Sky*, 2015

resetting the bones
of the fence—
morning glory vines

 ~*Chad Lee Robinson,* The Deep End of the Sky, *2015*

my grandmother's Bible–
every bookmark
an obituary

 ~*Chad Lee Robinson,* The Deep End of the Sky, *2015*

Mother's Day
her apron
now her bib

 ~*Patricia Rogers,* in N. M. Sola, ed. *Four Hundred and Two Snails: HSA Members' Anthology, 2018*

salsa music
   on the hot sand
      grandma dances

  ~*Susan Rogers*

just after midnight
   his grandmother's face
         in the window

  ~*Susan Rogers*

after all these years
deep inside the window seat
the lost wedding band

  ~*Susan Rogers*

holding hands
we watch the fields
turn gold

   ~*Susan Rogers*

Gnarled
winter rhododendron—
I, too, am old

   ~*David H. Rosen, Spelunking Through Life, 2016*

Tree watching
I see a bird . . .
memories of childhood

   ~*David H. Rosen and Johnny Baranski, White Rose, Red Rose, 2017*

Holding hands
our age spots
Kiss

> ~ David H. Rosen and Johnny Baranski, *White Rose, Red Rose*, 2017

Handicapped grey beard rounding the pond

> ~ David H. Rosen, *Torii Haiku: Profane to a Sacred Life*, 2018

Old oaks
bend
toward the sun

> ~ David H. Rosen, *Torii Haiku: Profane to a Sacred Life*, 2018

cataract removed
spotting the pigeon
with one red toe

~Sydell Rosenberg

In the library
   discussing their stocks and bonds:
      senior citizens.

~Sydell Rosenberg, *Modern Haiku,* 4.3, 1973

New York Miniature

Watching them cement
broken city streets with sweat,
withered idle men
commenting on the right way
in the summer afternoon.

~Sydell Rosenberg, *Skylark Tanka Journal,*
6:2, 2018

On the first warm day
   the old lady tells her tales
      from start to finish.

  ~*Sydell Rosenberg*

old stone Buddha
up to his hips with moss
end of summer ...

  ~*Bruce Ross, Frogpond,* 41:2, 2018

*Eat everything
on your plate,
I tell my elderly mother.*

  ~*Alexis Rotella, Ouch: Senryu,* 2007

During dinner,
he tells us
we're not in his will.

   ~Alexis Rotella, Ouch: Senryu, 2007

Seventy-second birthday
my 86-year-old friend
looks younger than me

   ~Alexis Rotella

Another hearing aid flyer
my husband
won't hear of it

   ~Alexis Rotella

They get married
in sweats—
the 80-year olds.

~*Alexis Rotella, Ouch: Senryu, 2007*

liver spots . . .
my granddaughter's voice
1...3...2...4...12

~*Margaret Rutley and Sidney Bending*

syncopation
the old man's hip
and the rocking chair

~*Margaret Rutley and Sidney Bending*

first date jitters
he jitterbugs
into his girdle

~ *Margaret Rutley and Sidney Bending*

small talk
I remember you when
you were this big

~ Tom Sacramona, *Frogpond,* 42:1, 2019

rinsing sand
off her feet
and cane

~ *Tom Sacramona, New England Letters,* #75, 2017

mountain climbing,
getting steeper from here—
my midlife

~*Ernesto P. Santiago*

keeping well
in the winter cold
a tattered coat

~*Ernesto P. Santiago*

bathing
in equal light
an old frog

~*Ernesto P. Santiago*

becoming old
in both hands - the lightness
of a butterfly

   ~Ernesto P. Santiago

handsomely,
growing old without knowing—
a laughing mountain

   ~Ernesto P. Santiago

childhood village
my reflection at the bottom
of an old well

   ~Agnes Eva Savich

light breeze
falling blossoms mingle
with my first grays

~*Agnes Eva Savich*

early spring
great-grandma's grin
from the tree house

~*Agnes Eva Savich, Asahi Haikuist Network,*
2018

reunion bonfire
a hush as the elders
recall their elders

~*Agnes Eva Savich, Presence, #55, 2016*

in the dark we are ageless shooting stars

~*Agnes Eva Savich, Under the Basho*, 2015

I remember
your braid —
girl gone to soldier

~*Miriam Sagan, All My Beautiful Failures*, 2013

purple allium
full of bees — we've been friends
these almost thirty years

~*Miriam Sagan, All My Beautiful Failures*, 2013

footprints in snow
crescent moon, all my
beautiful failures

~ *Miriam Sagan, All My Beautiful Failures*, 2013

my grandparents' home
only black and white photos
on the walls

~ *Vessislava Savova*

old movies
my grandfather's medals
from WWII

~ *Vessislava Savova*

lily of the valley
tea and cookies
with my grandma

   ~*Vessislava Savova*

back home
my father's rocking chair
still by the window

   ~*Vessislava Savova*

phoning my aged mother...
the time it takes her
to answer

   ~*Olivier Schopfer, Prune Juice, #24, 2018*

tennis elbow
no longer
on the ball

> ~*Olivier Schopfer*, in J. Kacian, ed. *Haiku in the Workplace*, 2017

work from home
too old
for homework

> ~*Olivier, Schopfer*, in J. Kacian, ed. *Haiku in the Workplace*, 2017

our song
on the radio
twenty again

> ~*Olivier Schopfer*, in S. d'Andrea, ed. *Le Lumachine*, 28, 2018

winter morning
a soft-boiled egg
brings my childhood back to life

   ~*Olivier Schopfer*, in S. d'Andrea, ed. *Le Lumachine*, 28, 2018

another spring
both ends of the leash
slower

   ~*Ann K. Schwader, Frogpond*, 42.1, 2019

grey wedding
a crust sopping
with grape

   ~*Dan Schwerin*

older this morning
the fence takes up
with a vine

 ~*Dan Schwerin, ⊕RS*, 2015

over the hill
I hear a river
give up winter

 ~*Dan Schwerin, ⊕RS*, 2015

filed under miscellaneous the will to live

 ~*Shloka Shankar*

wormhole the time it takes to remember

～*Shloka Shankar, Under the Basho, 2016*

rain check   the shelf life of opportunities

～*Shloka Shankar, Frameless Sky, #7, 2017*

erecting landmarks in the field of why

～*Shloka Shankar, Under the Basho, 2018*

a solitary star
burns brighter
than the rest...
the story of my life
in these constellations

～*Shloka Shankar, Moonbathing, #11, 2014*

family reunion
extra salt
and vinegar

   ~ *Tiffany Shaw-Diaz, The Heron's Nest*, 19, 2017

half my life gone the violence of mating butterflies

   ~ *Sandra Simpson, The Heron's Nest,* 18, 2016

family photo box
how my father smiles
in black and white

   ~ *Sandra Simpson*, With Words Haiku Contest; Highly Commended, 2010

turning forty
still rewriting
the first page

   ~Caroline Skanne

this
meandering
river . . .
suddenly I feel too old
not to dream

   ~Caroline Skanne

tearful
for no apparent
reason . . .
I choose the teacup
with the most chips

   ~Caroline Skanne

spring rain all it takes to remember

  ~*Caroline Skanne*

equinox wind
the usual obsession
with mortality –
deep in the yellow woods
leaves fall into silence

  ~*Caroline Skanne, Moonbathing, #19, 2018*

naked grandchildren
run through the house
the old dog sleeps

  ~*d w skrivseth, nameless: haiku and senryu,*
  2018

first morning
washing my bowl
with last year's water

    ~*d w skrivseth, nameless: haiku and senryu, 2018*

sixty-nine years old
little do I need
purple iris

    ~*d w skrivseth, nameless: haiku and senryu, 2018*

silver threads
in the bird's nest
going grey

    ~*Robin Anna Smith*

enduring ailment...
her husband loosens
his wedding vows

> ~*Robin Anna Smith*, in N. M. Sola, ed. *Four Hundred and Two Snails: HSA Members' Anthology*, 2018

a field of daisies growing from my pain

> ~*Robin Anna Smith, Under the Basho*, 2018

stifling summer–
more candles than breath
this birthday

> ~*Robin Anna Smith, Chrysanthemum*, 23, 2018

crayon portrait–
I color myself
young again

   ~*Robin Anna Smith, ephemarae*, 1A, 2018

embossed wedding ring
worn down paper thin and smooth
after sixty years

   ~*Val Smith*

my lively puppy
gave me love and devotion
over fifteen years

   ~*Val Smith*

magpies' dawn chorus
each year a new nest of young
add to my joy

   ~ Val Smith

my mother and aunt
get together ...
dueling walkers

   ~ Carmi Soifer

terns head in
toward shore
my friend's remaining days

   ~ Carmi Soifer

squirrels chasing
each other ...
I am still alive

~ *Carmi Soifer, The Heron's Nest*, 13, 2011

on the list
of deceased classmates
the friend
I'd always planned
to see again

~ *Sheila Sondik, a hundred gourds,* 1:2, 2012

laminated now
the typewritten recipe
I know by heart
still I consult its stained blur
when I crave her comfort food

~ *Sheila Sondik, Ribbons,* 13:3, 2017

all my devices
plugged in for the night
I'm free to dream
of the years I had babies
and no screens to nurture

> ~*Sheila Sondik*, Tanka Society of America
> Sanford Goldstein International Tanka
> Contest, 2017; Honorable Mention

newly in love
we hiked the high Sierras
forty-five years later
far below those soaring peaks
we walk countless clinic hallways

> ~*Sheila Sondik*, Fujisan Award Contest, 2018;
> Honorable Mention

my favorite
Shakespeare play
The Tempest
makes me nervous now—
must we give up our magic?

~ *Sheila Sondik, Gusts, #28, 2018*

old slippers
the comfort
coming apart

~ *John Stevenson, Some of the Silence, 1999*

one last look
through the old apartment
a dry sponge

~ *John Stevenson, quiet enough, 2004*

clear skies
the river dark
with old rain

   ~John Stevenson, Some of the Silence, 1999

our sleeping bags
the lingering scent
of old campfires

   ~John Stevenson, quiet enough, 2004

early Alzheimer's
she says she'll have . . .
the usual

   ~John Stevenson, quiet enough, 2004

catnap...
the creak of an old elm
as it sways

   ~Mike Stinson

Cardinal's song
I mourn a friend's
loss of hearing

   ~Mike Stinson

childhood prayer
"if I die before I wake"
revisited

   ~Mike Stinson

quite a spectacle
searching for the glasses
atop my head

 ~*Mike Stinson, cattails*, 2017

senior center
she propels her wheelchair
with baby steps

 ~*Mike Stinson*

the growth rings
of otoliths and trees . . .
when did she
become smaller
than her daughters

 ~*Debbie Strange*, Fleeting Words Tanka
  Competition, 2017; 2nd Place

golden years . . .
no one tells you about
the tarnish

~ *Debbie Strange, Prune Juice, #26, 2018*

~*Debbie Strange, Failed Haiku, #36, 2018*

~ *Debbie Strange, cattails*, 2017

~Debbie Strange, *Blithe Spirit*, 28.2, 2018

the long throw
of a smoothly worn stone
dying, we live

~Alan Summers, *hedgerow, #23*, 2016

I start to rain
and into falling leaves
my childhood

>~*Alan Summers*, The Haiku Foundation;
>Sense of Place, 2018

childhood river the sunlight as it falls

>~*Alan Summers, Presence,* #62, 2018

working the ice cream
we walk all the way back
to yesterday

>~*Alan Summers, Notes from the Gean*, #21,
>2013

electrical storms
the Methuselah star finds
its birth certificate

   ~*Alan Summers, Scope*, 60: 3, 2014

winter breeze
he's trying to
blow out 72 candles

   ~ *Agus Maulana Sunjaya, Failed Haiku*, #28, 2018

winter ends
finally, my daughter
calls me 'daddy'

   ~*Agus Maulana Sunjaya, Poetry Pea*, 2018

midday rain
the smile on the face
of an old Jizo

    ~*Agus Maulana Sunjaya*

a strand of white
in my mother's head
first snow

    ~*Agus Maulana Sunjaya*

broken window
the grin of
my toothless nanny

    ~*Agus Maulana Sunjaya, Failed Haiku, #28, 2018*

another year
still this scar
reminds me

   ~*Rachel Sutcliffe,*
    brass bell, 2017

old wallpaper
the peeling layers
of life

   ~*Rachel Sutcliffe, Frogpond,* 42:1, 2019

an urban lake
the memory of the ancestors
in silver glow

   ~*Minko Tanev*

mummer masks –
pagan symbols
on the day of forgiveness

~Minko Tanev

older marriage
the gentle choreography
of breakfast

~Hilary Tann, The Heron's Nest, 18, 2016

reunion
too old to be young again
the class clown

~Barbara Tate,
www.charlottedigregorio.wordpress.com

chemo
the passport photo
no longer me

   ~*Barabara Tate*, H. Gene Murtha Senryu
   Competition; Honorable Mention, 2018

lapping a puddle
of last night's rain
...the old cat

   ~*Barbara Tate*

mustard seed
I teach my old dog
a new trick

   ~*Barbara Tate*

Veteran's Day
young again he salutes
the flag

   ~*Barbara Tate*

morning rain
the fading dream
of my first love

   ~*Dietmar Tauchner, Frogpond,* 41.3, 2018

one year older
the growing number
of keys on my bunch

   ~*Dietmar Tauchner, hedgerow,* 2018

The open journal
remembering being sixteen
same handwriting

~ *Katya Sabaroff Taylor,*
brass bell, 2017

My pen doesn't care
how old my hand is – I write
to salvage the world

~ *Katya Sabaroff Taylor, My Haiku Life,* 2009

63rd birthday—
we remember it
for her

~ *Stacy Taylor; for Liz Kamens*

silver hair. . .
a saint's eyes help me
break free

   ~ Diana Teneva

once too slow
& now too fast
the old sledding hill

   ~ vincent tripi, to what none of us knows, 2012

was breast-fed . . .
   some snow on
      the old boathouse doors

   ~ vincent tripi, to what none of us knows, 2012

my old typewriter . . .
   the "i" key
      feels like all the rest

  ~*vincent tripi, to what none of us knows,* 2012

Lady's slipper & i . . .
   lied about
      my age

  ~*vincent tripi, to what none of us knows,* 2012

between the robin and
earthworm 70th spring

  ~*vincent tripi, to what none of us knows,* 2012

love in middle age
moonlight
on a white iris

   ~ Charles Trumbull, The Orb Weaver's Web, 2010

Russian tango records—
the old spy's eyes gently close
as he hums along

   ~ Charles Trumbull

whatnot shop
she buys an old photo
of somebody's wedding

   ~ Charles Trumbull

commencement day:
graduates and old folks
dream, swapping roles

~*Charles Trumbull*

sandstone formation
an old Navajo woman
bends into the wind

~*Charles Trumbull, A Five-Balloon Morning,*
2013

it's happened!
we must be truly old . . .
sounds
of our neighbour shoveling
our driveway

~*Naomi Beth Wakan*

I grow old
impatient with words
which can explain nothing
"what is left to do?" I ask . . .
the wind blows up from the beach

  ~*Naomi Beth Wakan*

reading the obituaries
I absent-mindedly stroke
my liver-spotted hands

  ~*Naomi Beth Wakan*

this world's a mess
it's time to go and yet . . .
spring blossom

~Naomi Beth Wakan

the last act!
I thought this was
the dress rehearsal!

~Naomi Beth Wakan

another sunrise
of holiness
two old goats

~ *Miriam Wald*

those final years
the drool on dad's shirt
a droplet on my journal

> ~*Diane Wallihan,* in N. M. Sola, ed. *Four Hundred and Two Snails: HSA Members' Anthology,* 2018

leaning into the wind
on a windless day
the old couple

> ~*Diane Wallihan, Modern Haiku,* 47.1, 2016

his droopy pants
his hunched shoulders
she calls him 'handsome'

> ~*Diane Wallihan*

seniors in wellies —
proving their power
puddle to puddle

~*Diane Wallihan*

change in focus —
threading a needle
by faith

~*Julie Warther, Prune Juice, #18, 2016*

cataract clouds . . .
her children remind her
what she likes

~*Julie Warther, tinywords, #15:2, 2015*

splitting pills
for the arthritic dog –
autumn equinox

~*Julie Warther, The Heron's Nest,* 19, 2017

memories leaving no tracks through the snow

~*Julie Warther, A Hundred Gourds,* 5.1, 2015

all the king's horses
accepting
my new normal

~*Julie Warther,* HPNC Senryu Contest, 2018; Honorable Mention

Old plastic flowers
cracked, dusty, faded
poked into dry pots

~Kathy Waters

Childhood scars fading
beneath newly plowed wrinkles
what will spring from this earth?

~Kathy Waters

Am I going gray
or is silvered moonlight
shimmering my hair?

~Kathy Waters

Polka dot boxer shorts
jog past, defiant graybeard
passes gravestones with ease

~Kathy Waters

watch hands
no fingers
pointing to time

~Roger Watson, Blithe Spirit, 27: 3, 2017

scrolling down
to my age group…
…the last

~Roger Watson, ephemerae, 1: A, 2018

antique shop
the smell
of opportunity

   ~ Roger Watson, ephemerae, 1:C, 2018

old soldier
with dull eyes
and glinting medals

   ~ Roger Watson

the old couple
with no words
left between them

   ~ Roger Watson

post-vasectomy,
this 'primal' urge
to overpunctuate

> ~Lew Watts, in N. M. Sola, ed. *Four Hundred and Two Snails: HSA Members' Anthology*, 2018

fortieth birthday—
I used to think nothing
of taking off my socks

> ~Michael Dylan Welch, *Frogpond*, 31:3, 2008

old folks' home—
the square of light
crosses the room

> ~Michael Dylan Welch, in M. Welch, ed. *Harvest: The Haiku North America Anthology*, 1991

old dog's cough
the color of
strawberries

> ~*Sharon R. Wesoky*, in N. M. Sola, ed. *Four Hundred and Two Snails: HSA Members' Anthology,* 2018

old family recipe
hoping our hands
are the same size

> ~*Johana West, The Heron's Nest*, 20, 2018

thistledown
on the wind...
when we were young

> ~*Lucy Whitehead, Otata* 31, 2018

smooth coin
the way time wears
our faces

    ~*Lucy Whitehead*, The Haiku Foundation, C. Kittner, Guest ed., 2019

dictaphone
the voice of a woman
I used to be

    ~*Lucy Whitehead,* The Haiku Foundation, C. Kittner, Guest ed., 2019

paleolithic handprint   the span of a life

    ~*Lucy Whitehead, Otata*, 33, 2018

shooting star
how far the rest
of our journey

~*Lucy Whitehead, Stardust Haiku, 17, 2018*

black varnish
hidden petroglyphs
come into view

~*Scott Wiggerman*

creaking vigas
in a Taos motel
dreams of old growth

~*Scott Wiggerman*

flash of coyote
then a second dash—
another birthday

~*Scott Wiggerman*

sere brown veins
of a curled leaf—
grandmother

~*Scott Wiggerman*

worn-down soles
on a well-trod path:
year's end

~*Scott Wiggerman, cattails*, 2014

the high bridge
from here the sea
shows its age

～*Ian Willey, The Heron's Nest, 18, 2016*

a weathered haiku
all that remains of the poet
swaying on a branch

～*Margo Williams*

watercolor painting
hanging on the wall
her memory

～*Margo Williams*

another turn
around the sun
only this time alone

~*Margo Williams*

arthritic hand
still manages to pen
his last words

~*Margo Williams*

all that remains
framed brushstrokes
—grandchildren too

~*Margo Williams*

yellow caterpillar
your sticky crawl
from then to now
you'd think
I would have flown

~*Kath Abela Wilson, Bright Stars* #6, 2014

two old sisters
their strange lives
overhead
a creaky step that told
we were no different

~*Kath Abela Wilson, Bright Stars*, #6, 2014

I used to have an age
now I've lost it
completely
those squares I skipped
in my hopscotch days

~*Kath Abela Wilson, Bright Stars*, #6, 2014

nuclear family
fifty years later still
his fallout

> ~Kath Abela Wilson, in C. Hall, ed. *but for their voices*, 2014

between whatshisname
and whatshamacallit
the golden key

> ~Kath Abela Wilson, *Failed Haiku*, #23, 2017

an act of faith—
lending a beloved book
to a friend with dementia

> ~Fran Witham, *bottle rockets*, #31, 2014

losing her mind—
watching a woman
as she watches herself

   ~*Fran Witham, bottle rockets*, #31, 2014

geriatric psych ward—
an ashen-faced woman
her eyes averted
passes by me
taking baby steps

   ~*Fran Witham, bottle rockets*, #28, 2013

my aging father
building a birdhouse
his sandpaper voice

   ~*Robert Witmer,* in L. Gorman, ed. *On Down the Road: The HSA Members' Anthology,* 2017

cleaning out the kids' old room
that fairy tale
I never read

    ~Robert Witmer, Taj Mahal Review, 15:1, 2016

spring rain
old women bent over
their watercolors

    ~Robert Witmer, Frogpond, 35:2, 2012

a young man photographs
an old man painting
a flowering plum

    ~Robert Witmer, World Haiku Review, 2015

second childhood
the setting sun
on a ferris wheel

   ~ *Robert Witmer, Failed Haiku,* #16, 2017

late summer breeze
noticing the gray
in her muzzle

   ~ *Karina M. Young, The Heron's Nest,* 19, 2017;
   also in *Eucalyptus Wind,* 2017

last night
dreaming myself young again
brown hair below my waist

   ~ *Zee Zahava*

my memory house
every window opens to
yesterday

~Zee Zahava

how many years
since we crossed this bridge together
only my footprints now

~Zee Zahava

tomorrow
i'll be a child again
moon-dancing

~Zee Zahava

Glossary

Colace is a stool softener used to help facilitate softer bowel movements.

Dresden, a city located in eastern Germany and the capital of Saxony, was the site of terrible Allied bombing in 1945.

Homo naledi (meaning Star Man) refers to an extinct species of humans discovered in 2013 in the Rising Star cave in South Africa.

Jisei is a haiku written on one's deathbed, which may be considered, according to Buddhist scholar, Yoel Hoffmann, the poet's spiritual legacy.

Jizo refers to an enlightened being who is often depicted as a Buddhist monk.

Kibitizing refers to casual chatting, but it can also mean unsolicited advice as in a card game.

Mummer masks refers to the masks (and headgear) worn by troupes of local male amateur actors who hide their identity while performing during the 12 days before Christmas in Newfoundland, Ireland and parts of the United Kingdom.

Sakura refers to the cherry tree, which is renowned for its fragrant, beautiful blossoms.

Syrah, also known as Shiraz, is a red wine made from a black wine grape.

Viagra is a brand name prescription medication to enhance sexual potency in older adults.

Vigas is a rough-hewn timber that is often found in an adobe dwelling.

Yozakura refers to the Japanese tradition of nighttime viewing of cherry blossoms.

Recommended Reading

Brandt, A. *Mindful Aging: Embracing Your Life After 50 to Find Fulfillment, Purpose, and Joy.* Eua Claire, WI: Pesi Publishing & Media, 2017.

Dass, R. *Still Here: Embracing Aging, Changing and Dying.* New York, NY: Riverhead Books, 2000.

Epstein, R. *Nothing is Empty: A Whole Haiku World.* West Union, WV: Middle Island Press, 2019.

_____. *Turning the Page to Old: Haiku & Senryu.* West Union, WV: Middle Island Press, 2019.

_____. *Healing into Haiku: On Illness and Pain.* West Union, WV: Middle Island Press, 2018.

Epstein, R. and Taylor, S. *Suffering Buddha: The Zen Way Beyond Health and Illness.* Bloomington, IN: Trafford Publishing, 2010.

Erikson, E. *The Life Cycle Completed.* New York, NY: Norton, 1982.

Fessler, M. *Also.* Kanagawa, Japan: Kanuma House, 2019.

Gerson, M. *Listening to Midlife: Turning Your Crisis into a Quest.* Boston, MA: Shambhala Publications, 2009.

Hollis, J. *Finding Meaning in the Second Half of Life.* New York, NY: Gotham Books, 2009.

Jenkins, J. *Disrupt Aging: A Bold New Path to Living Your Best Life at Every Age.* New York, NY: Public Affairs, 2016.

Jung, C. G. "The Stages of Life" in *Modern Man in Search of a Soul.* W. S. Dell and Cary F. Baynes, tr. New York, NY: Harcourt Brace Jovanovich, 1933.

Kornfield, J. *No Time Like the Present: Finding Freedom, Love, and Joy Right Where You Are.* New York, NY: Atria, 2017.

Lao Tzu. *Tao Te Ching.* S. Mitchell, tr. New York, NY: HarperCollins Publishers, 1988.

Levine, S. *Healing into Life and Death.* Great Neck, NY: Doubleday, 1987.

Moore, T. *Ageless Soul: The Lifelong Journey Toward Meaning and Joy.* New York, NY: St. Martin's Press, 2017.

Richmond, L. *Aging as a Spiritual Practice: A Contemplative Guide to Growing Older and Wiser.* New York, NY: Gotham Books, 2012.

Rilke, R. M. *Letters on Life.* U. Baer, ed. New York, NY: Modern Library, 2005.

Sarton, M. *At Eighty-two: A Journal.* New York, NY: W. W. Norton & Co., 1966.

Sawin, L., Corbett, L., and Carbine, M., eds. *Jung and Aging: Possibilities and Potentials for the Second Half of Life.* New Orleans, LA: Spring Journal Books, 2014.

Schacter-Salomi, Z. *From Age-ing to Sage-ing: A Revolutionary Approach to Growing Older.* New York, NY: Warner Books, 1995.

Singh, K. D. *The Grace in Aging: Awaken as You Grow Older.* Boston: Wisdom Publications, 2014.

Suzuki, S. *Zen Mind, Beginner's Mind: Informal Talks on Zen Meditation and Practice.*

T. Dixon, ed. New York, NY: Weatherhill, Inc., 1970.

Thomas, W. H. *What Are Old People For? How Elders Will Save the World.* Acton, MA: Wander Wyk and Burnham, 2004.

Wakan, N. B. *A Roller-Coaster Ride: Thoughts on Aging.* Ontario, Canada: Wolsak and Wynn Publishers, 2012.

Weil, A. *Healthy Aging: A Lifelong Guide to Your Well Being.* New York, NY: Alfred A. Knopf, 2005.

Yalom, I. D. *Staring at the Sun: Overcoming the Terror of Death.* San Francisco, CA: Jossey-Bass, 2008.

www.ingramcontent.com/pod-product-compliance
Lightning Source LLC
Chambersburg PA
CBHW071652160426
43195CB00012B/1433